Answers to Fascinating Questions About the World Around You

By the Staff and Writers at LifesLittleMysteries.com

Compiled and Edited by Jerry Ropelato and Emily Sanderson

FOREWORD

Have you ever seen a news story on TV or in the newspaper that left you with unanswered questions? Did you ever wonder about something that you never got around to looking up? *Life's Little Mysteries* was designed to satisfy your curiosity. First as an online magazine and now compiled in this little book, we answer 115 questions on a variety of subjects.

Perhaps your child is in the "Why" stage of life: "Daddy, why do fireflies light up?" or "Mommy, why is Daddy bald?" Grade-schoolers may have different questions, such as, "What causes the tides?" or "What's it like to live in space?" As a certified source of knowledge about all mysteries, you'd better know the answers for your kids, and we can help. Designed for families, this book is fun to share aloud with human beings of all ages.

We find that an answer to one question often spurs new ones, so our book provides answers to some questions you may not have thought of, such as "Why don't woodpeckers get headaches?" and "What are the best MacGyver stunts?" Our answers are meant to entertain while they inform, and they are sure to provoke at least an occasional chuckle. Enjoy this book on a lazy afternoon on your back porch, begin conversations at a party with it, or use it in the classroom.

Did curiosity really kill the cat? We don't think so. If you have a question that isn't answered in this book, visit the *Life's Little Mysteries* website at www.LifesLittleMysteries.com.

Sincerely,
Jerry Ropelato
CEO, TechMediaNetwork

s a child, did you ever receive a chemistry set, an ant farm or a box of tinker toys as a birthday present? Perhaps stargazing was your thing. No matter what our hobbies, some of us never get past the "Why" stage in life. And some of the most successful people in this world have been willing to ask the question "Why not?" When we know more about why the world is the way it is, we are more apt to recognize patterns and make connections. This book is dedicated to all of you dreamers with inquisitive minds.

I'd also like to thank all those who have contributed to this book, who are dreamers themselves. They include Emily Sanderson, my editor and the person who has done all of the legwork in making this book possible; Robert Roy Britt, editor-in-chief and founder of LifesLittleMysteries.com; Jared Page and Bryan Green who contributed to the book's design; and *Life's Little Mysteries* contributors including Robert Roy Britt, Amber Angelle, Molika Ashford, Michael Avila, Corey Binns, Jeanna Bryner, Michelle Bryner, Bjorn Carey, Albert Ching, Lauren Cox, Denise Chow, Stuart Fox, Nicholas Gerbis, Kristina Grifantini, Adam Hadhazy, Zoe Macintosh, Ben Mauk, Remy Melina, Lily Norton, Stephanie Pappas, Dan Peterson, Benjamin Radford, Karen Rowan, Greg Soltis, Andrea Thompson and Heather Whipps. They have gone beyond the call of duty to research educational and entertaining content, and they have all played an integral role in making the book what it has become today.

Table of Contents

Chapter 1
Body and Mind

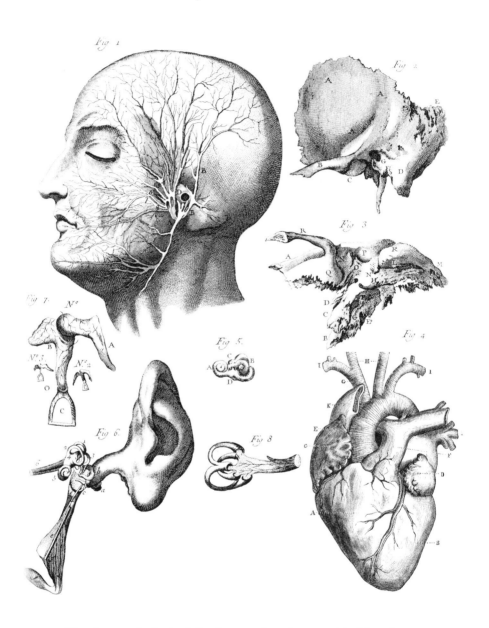

The human body is full of mysteries that mankind has been trying to understand since the beginning of time. In this chapter, we provide some modern-day answers.

Do People Really Use Just 10 Percent of Their Brains?

he brain is an amazing thing. Our brains help us learn, create, and imagine, and often it seems that there's almost nothing that our magical three pounds of neurons can't do. But many People believe we only use 10 percent of our brains. In fact, some claim that people with extrasensory perception (ESP) are merely able to use more of their brains than other people. After all, imagine what we could do by tapping into the other 90 percent we're not using!

Unfortunately for those who believe this idea, the 10 percent figure is a myth. In fact people use all of their brains. Researchers using brain imaging research techniques, such as positron emission tomography (PET) scans and functional magnetic resonance imaging (fMRI), have found that brain scans clearly show that the entire brain is used, according to Barry Beyerstein, a professor of psychology at Simon Fraser University who has studied the myth for years.

> THE FACT IS, PEOPLE USE ALL OF THEIR BRAINS. IT'S TRUE THAT PEOPLE DON'T USE ALL PARTS OF THEIR BRAINS AT THE SAME TIME, JUST AS PEOPLE DON'T USE ALL OF THEIR BODY MUSCLES AT THE SAME TIME.

It's true that people don't use all parts of their brain at the same time, just as people don't use all of their body muscles at the same time. But throughout the various activities of an average day, all brain areas are used.

"The last century has witnessed the advent of increasingly sophisticated technologies for snooping in the brain's traffic," says Scott Lilienfeld in *50 Great Myths of Popular Psychology: Shattering Widespread Misconceptions about Human Behavior*. "Despite this detailed mapping, no quiet areas awaiting new assignments have emerged. In fact, even simple tasks generally require contributions of processing areas spread throughout virtually the whole brain.''

The "10 percent myth'' suggests that most of the brain is just waiting to be used. But if parts of the brain were unused, the effects of damaging those parts should be minor. Yet people who have suffered head trauma, a stroke or other brain injury can be severely impaired.

So use your brain and don't believe this myth!

by Benjamin Radford

Is Walking to School Good for Kids?

e've all heard it from our grandparents but never believed it when they said, "Why, when I was your age, I walked to school every day in the snow, and it was uphill both ways!''

Still, many of us can remember the days of walking to school. But with growing suburbs, the lack of sidewalks and safety concerns, the bus and the car are the most common way to get to school these days, and researchers at the University at Buffalo in New York say that change can have a significant effect on students' health and even stress levels.

In a new study, researchers at the University of Buffalo designed an experiment that involved 20 boys and 20 girls between the ages of 10 and 14. To simulate a ride to school, they asked half of them to sit in a comfortable chair for 10 minutes while suburban scenes flashed by on surrounding screens. The other 20 students watched the same images, but they spent the 10 minutes walking on a treadmill with a full backpack

About 20 minutes after "arriving'' to school, the students took what's called a Stroop test. The names of colors are printed on a card in a different color (for example, the word "red'' is printed in blue ink), and students were asked to identify the written word.

During the test, the pulses of the walkers increased three beats per minute while the riders' heartbeats rose 11 beats per minute. Systolic blood pressure was three times higher, and perceived stress was twice as high in the riders.

The increase in stress is important because cardiovascular disease can begin early in life, from the elevated pulse and blood pressure that result from stress. Known as cardiovascular reactivity, this condition begins the process of atherosclerosis, which clogs artery walls with cholesterol, calcium and other bad stuff.

CARDIOVASCULAR DISEASE CAN BEGIN WHILE YOU'RE YOUNG. FREQUENT EXERCISE PERFORMED EARLY IN THE DAY CAN HELP TO REDUCE STRESS WHICH CONTRIBUTES TO THE DISEASE.

"The cardiovascular disease process begins in childhood, so if we can find some way of stopping or slowing that process, that would provide an important health benefit," says study researcher James Roemmich, associate professor of pediatrics and exercise at the university. "We know that physical activity has a protective effect on the development of cardiovascular disease, and one way it may be doing so is by reducing stress reactivity."

At first, this may seem like another study promoting the benefits of exercise for kids. The interesting twist is the timing of the walk to school. An early morning jaunt prepares students for the first part of the day, which may last awhile before recess.

"[Walking] puts them in a constantly protective state against stressors that they're incurring during the school day, whether that be taking an exam, trying to fit in with peers or speaking in front of classmates," Roemmich says. The research was published in the journal *Medicine & Science in Sports & Exercise*.

So, hand them their backpack and some good shoes, and point them towards school in the morning. Hopefully, the journey is uphill in only one direction.

by Dan Peterson

Can You Really Laugh Until You Cry?

e laugh in joy and cry over pain, right? Well, it turns out that it's not so black and white. Although not fully understood, we can laugh until we cry. Both laughing and crying happen during times of high emotion, University of Maryland at Baltimore psychologist Robert Provine tells Prevention.com. There's also evidence that the same part of the brain is responsible for both crying and laughing. In fact, lesions on certain regions of the brain have been linked to a syndrome called pathological laughter and crying (PLC), which is characterized by uncontrollable outbursts of these two expressions. The fact that the same lesion causes both tears and laughter suggests they are linked somehow, according to the PBS special, "The Adult Brain."

Another explanation points to pressure being put on the tear ducts as a result of a body-shaking, vigorous laugh. These tears are considered reflex tears because they result from external factors, such as an airborne irritant or the wind, and not due to emotion.

Emotional tears have a different chemical makeup than reflex teardrops, according to research by William Frey, professor at the University of Minnesota. The emotion-driven water drops contain more of certain hormones, including leucine enkephalin, a natural painkiller.

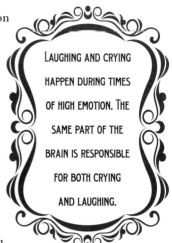

LAUGHING AND CRYING HAPPEN DURING TIMES OF HIGH EMOTION. THE SAME PART OF THE BRAIN IS RESPONSIBLE FOR BOTH CRYING AND LAUGHING.

by Michelle Bryner

What Is the Funny Bone?

 ven a light tap to the back of your elbow can send pain shooting down your forearm. You've hit the spot, your funny bone. Turns out, this spot is neither "funny" nor a "bone." In fact, you've just hit your ulnar nerve, which controls feeling in your pinky and ring fingers, and it helps control the muscles in the wrist, as well as parts of the hand.

This nerve travels from your neck down your upper arm, wrapping around the elbow joint on its way to the hand. In most spots along this route the ulnar nerve stays hidden within muscles and other tissue. But when it passes through your elbow joint, the nerve is particularly close to the skin—making it a vulnerable target.

THE PATIENT IN THE CHILDREN'S GAME OPERATION BY MILTON BRADLEY HAS A FUNNY BONE.

One idea for how the ulnar nerve got its silly name is the fact that the nerve also runs through the humerus bone in your upper arm. No joke.

by Michelle Bryner

What Is the Strongest Muscle in the Human Body?

hether we're babies or body builders, we all have muscles. They grow, they bulge, they stretch and sometimes they even painfully pull. But for all the work they do for us, we are still unable to crown one as "the strongest muscle."

Instead, a few muscles could claim the title, depending on how strength is measured.

If the title goes to the muscle that can exert the most force, the victor would be the soleus, or the calf muscle, according to *Gray's Anatomy*, the anatomy textbook. Without this muscle, we wouldn't be able to stand, walk, run or shake our bodies on the dance floor. If the soleus was not continuously pulling, we would always be falling over ourselves (although some of us tend to do that from time to time anyway).

> SOME MUSCLES CAN EXERT QUICK BURSTS OF FORCE OR PRESSURE. SOME ARE VERSATILE. OTHERS, LIKE THE HEART, NEVER STOP WORKING THROUGHOUT YOUR LIFETIME.

But perhaps the title should go to the muscle that exerts the most pressure. Pressure is different from force—pressure takes into account the area over which a force is exerted. The muscle that takes the prize for delivering the greatest amount of pressure is the masseter, or the jaw muscle, according to the book *Clinical Oral Science*.

In 1986, Richard Hofmann of Lake City, Fla., achieved a bite strength of 975 pounds (442 kg) for two seconds, setting a Guinness Record. Talk about jaw dropping! The jaw is able to clench and chew because of the masseter muscle.

Others may argue the muscles used in childbirth are the most powerful. To be specific, the ability of the myometrium, or the uterine muscle, to contract and relax makes human birth possible. But because these muscles are not often used and are highly dependent on an interaction of hormonal and biochemical factors, some discount the myometrium as the strongest muscle.

When it comes to versatility, perhaps the tongue is the strongest muscle. Its combination of elasticity and forcefulness gives us the ability to speak, eat and kiss— all things very desirable on a first date. However dexterous it may be though, the tongue's power does not match that of muscles such as the soleus.

If slow and steady wins the race, the heart is certainly a contender for the title. Electrical impulses in the myocardium, the heart's muscular wall, keep your heart beating. When it contracts, the muscle pumps about two ounces (59 milliliters) of blood and is constantly working over a lifetime. Beating about 40 million times a year, a person's heart will beat approximately 2.5 billion times by the time of their 70th birthday.

THE ROBUST MYOMETRIUM ALLOWS THE UTERUS TO CONTRACT AND RELAX, MAKING CHILDBIRTH POSSIBLE. BUT SOME DISCOUNT THE MUSCLE'S STRENGTH IN COMPARISON WITH OTHER MUSCLES BECAUSE IT IS ASSISTED BY A NUMBER OF HORMONAL AND BIOCHEMICAL FACTORS, WHICH ALSO PLAY A SIGNIFICANT ROLE IN THE BIRTHING PROCESS.

by Lily Norton

How Loud Can You Play Music Without Damaging Your Hearing?

f you're listening to Katy Perry or the Red Hot Chili Peppers and have to raise your voice to be heard over the music, it's time to turn the volume down. Listening to loud music for too long can damage sensitive structures in the inner ear and lead to permanent hearing loss.

> BE ON THE LOOKOUT FOR SIGNS THAT THE TUNES YOU'VE BEEN LISTENING TO ARE TOO LOUD. YOU MAY NOTICE SOUNDS ARE MUFFLED AND THAT IT'S HARDER TO HEAR. YOU MAY ALSO FEEL PRESSURE OR A BLOCKED SENSATION, AND RINGING IN THE EAR.

Today one in five American teens already have some hearing loss, according to a recent study published in the *Journal of the American Medical Association*. That's a 30 percent increase from 15 years ago.

A person exposed to noise levels at 85 decibels or higher for a prolonged period of time is at risk for hearing loss. You shouldn't listen to music, or be exposed to any noise, at 85 decibels for more than eight hours at a time, says Gordon Hughes, program officer of clinical trials at the National Institute on Deafness and Other Communication Disorders (NIDCD). If you've got the volume cranked to 88 decibels, then cut your listening time down to four hours.

At its loudest, an MP3 player pumps out 105 decibels—that's 100 times more intense than 85 decibels. The trouble is, you may not feel any symptoms or know that you're putting your ears at risk. Young ears are more resilient than older ones.

"It's more difficult for kids to perceive the noxious effect of pollution noise," Hughes says.

What can you do to protect your hearing? "One way you can tell if your music is too loud is if you're talking to a friend and you have to raise your voice to be heard," Hughes says. Normal conversation is around 60 decibels. "That's a crude but helpful way to estimate whether ambient noise is too loud." You can do online research about your MP3 player to find where the 85-decibel mark is, and keep your volume turned below it.

A PERSON EXPOSED TO NOISE LEVELS AT 85 DECIBELS OR HIGHER FOR MORE THAN EIGHT HOURS AT A TIME IS AT RISK FOR HEARING LOSS.

At rock concerts, keeping your distance from the speakers and wearing some kind of protection can shield your ears. Inserts made of foam are the most common, says Hughes, but the least helpful. "They take the edge off." An ear muff, or protective head phone will also offer some quiet. But the best option is to get a custom fit ear mold that fits into your ear canal, which can cut down an estimated 60 decibels.

Be on the lookout for signs that the tunes you've been listening to are too loud. You may notice sounds are muffled and that it's harder to hear. You may also feel pressure or a blocked sensation, and ringing in the ear. "These are hallmarks of temporary hearing damage," Hughes says.

About 26 million Americans between the ages of 20 and 69 have lost the ability to hear high-frequencies from overexposure to loud noises at work or during leisure activities, like turning up their music too loud, according to the NIDCD.

"Prevention is really the name of the game," Hughes says. "Once you've got a hearing impairment from noise, the only thing you can do is consider a hearing aid."

by Corey Binns

Does the Heart Ever Skip a Beat?

here's nothing romantic about your heart skipping a beat, whatever a poet might say. All hearts flutter from time to time. These arrhythmias are generally harmless and may have no discernable cause at all. But if it happens frequently or is accompanied by other symptoms (like shortness of breath), the sight of your sweetie might not be to blame.

THE PIONEER COUNTRY SINGER BUCK OWENS IS FAMOUS FOR SINGING HIS 1966 HIT, "MY HEART SKIPS A BEAT."

Atrial fibrillation (AF), the most common affliction of the heart, affects over 2 million Americans. Those with the disorder have hearts whose upper chambers beat irregularly and too rapidly. AF can cause blood clots and is linked to one-third of all strokes in those over 65. It arises not from swooning or sneezing, but usually from infections or other heart disease.

There may also be a link between AF and alcohol consumption, excessive caffeine, stress and drug use. In some cases, an inherited genetic defect causes AF.

by Life's Little Mysteries *Staff*

What Is a Gluten-Free Diet?

Gluten is a protein found in wheat, barley and rye and is known to cause damage to the intestines of people with celiac disease.

In healthy people, the inside of the small intestine is lined with finger-like projections called villi. The main function of villi is to increase the surface area of the small intestine so that the nutrients in food can be better absorbed by the body.

> PEOPLE WHO HAVE CELIAC DISEASE CAN'T EAT FOODS THAT CONTAIN WHEAT, BARLEY OR RYE BECAUSE DOING SO CAN DAMAGE THEIR DIGESTIVE TRACTS.

In people with celiac disease, gluten irritates the lining of the small intestine and also causes the immune system to attack the villi. Over time, the villi can be damaged or destroyed. As a result, the inside of the small intestines are left more flattened than they should be, and the body is no longer able absorb enough nutrients from food. Nutrients pass through the digestive tract and are excreted with the body's waste, and the person can suffer malnutrition, according to WebMD.

> BREAD, CEREAL AND PASTA ARE OBVIOUS GLUTEN-RICH FOODS. BUT MARINADES THAT USE BARLEY-BASED ALCOHOL OR CANDY WITH MALTED INGREDIENTS CAN ALSO CAUSE A NEGATIVE REACTION.

Foods containing gluten are common. Bread, cereal and pasta are among the foods that people with celiac disease need to forgo, unless they have been specially formulated to be gluten-free.

Although some have suggested that a gluten-free diet may help alleviate the signs of autism in children, several scientific studies have now shown that the diet does not improve their behavior.

by Karen Rowan

Does Washing Lettuce Get Rid of Bacteria?

 recent recall of tainted romaine lettuce left many plates devoid of the crisp veggie. Washing produce, even very carefully, may not remove all the bacteria present, so recalls are necessary when certain supplies of vegetables may have been exposed to bacteria that could make us sick.

An estimated 76 million cases of food-borne disease occur each year in the United States, according to the CDC, and the bacteria that cause these illnesses, such as salmonella or *E. coli*, can hang on tight to food even through a washing.

"If you've got bacteria on the surface of fruits and vegetables, and you give them a wash with cold water, it removes some of what's on the surface," says Brendan Niemira of the USDA. "Unfortunately, it [cold water rinsing] doesn't remove all of them."

THE DELICATE, TINY RIDGES OF LETTUCE MAKE THE VEGETABLE DIFFICULT TO WASH THOROUGHLY. IF DISTRIBUTORS DISCOVER THAT IT HAS BEEN EXPOSED TO E. COLI OR OTHER HARMFUL BACTERIA, THEY WILL LIKELY RECALL IT FROM GROCERY STORES AND INFORM THE PUBLIC.

Rough surfaces, like those on cantaloupes and spinach, provide lots of nooks and crannies in which bacteria can hide out. Tomatoes are much smoother, though their surfaces do contain tiny pores that make homes for bacteria.

CONDITIONS FOR HARVESTING SAFE LETTUCE.

~ CLEAN IRRIGATION WATER

~ ABSENCE OF SOIL AMENDMENTS SUCH AS MANURE

~ CLEAN HANDS AND SHIPPING CONTAINERS

~ ANIMALS KEPT AWAY FROM LETTUCE FIELDS

SOURCE: USDA

"Most bacteria can't be washed off," agrees Doug Powell, associate professor of food safety at Kansas State University. And although it happens rarely, bacteria in soil can also be taken up by the roots of plants and remain inside the plant's veins, where they would be impossible to remove by washing.

"We need to make sure that the water is clean, that some soil amendments aren't used, that the hands and the shipping containers that come in contact with the crops are clean, and that animals are kept away," Powell says.

Although disease-causing bacteria are also found in meat, cooking kills the bacteria. "Fresh produce is a common source of outbreaks because it's eaten raw," Powell says.

by Jeanna Bryner and Karen Rowan

Is Sugar Bad for You?

 ome soda makers have recently switched from corn syrup to sugar to sweeten their soft drinks. The change was partly in response to a corn shortage but also because many people believe that sugar is healthier or more natural than high fructose corn syrup. On the other hand, countless products are advertised as "sugar free," and everyone agrees that people eat too much sugar.

So what's the deal? Is sugar bad for you or not? Sugar consumption has been associated with a variety of health problems ranging from dental cavities to obesity, but definitive links between sugar and ill health are difficult to make because sugary foods are often high in fat as well. Diets high in sugar tend to be unhealthy, but that does not necessarily mean that sugar itself is unhealthy.

> DESPITE POPULAR MYTHS ABOUT A "SUGAR HIGH," SUGAR HAS NOT BEEN LINKED TO HYPERACTIVITY IN CHILDREN. NOR DOES CONSUMPTION AFFECT THEIR COGNITIVE ABILITIES. HOWEVER, A HEALTHY MODERATION OF THE SWEET STUFF, AS WELL AS OTHER CARBOHYDRATES AND OTHER EMPTY CALORIES, WILL HELP PREVENT DISEASES SUCH AS DIABETES.

Many parents are cautious about giving their children candy, though despite popular myths about a "sugar high," sugar has not been linked to hyperactivity in children.

"Sugar does not affect the behavior or cognitive performance of children," conclude researchers who investigated a link between sugar and behavior in a study published in the *Journal of the American Medical Association*. Instead, the researchers found that the assumed link between sugar and hyperactivity "may be due to expectancy and common association."

Sugar is not necessarily bad for you, but, like salt, fat and other tasty ingredients, it should be consumed in moderation. Doing so is difficult, however, because much of the sugar that most Americans eat is "hidden." Everyone expects to find sugar in candy bars and soft drinks, but significant quantities of sugar can also be found in many common foods, from ketchup to salad dressings to pasta sauce. And, of course, there is naturally occurring sugar in many fruits and vegetables.

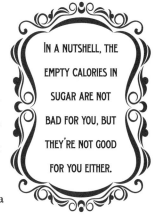

IN A NUTSHELL, THE EMPTY CALORIES IN SUGAR ARE NOT BAD FOR YOU, BUT THEY'RE NOT GOOD FOR YOU EITHER.

Because sugar contains no vitamins or minerals, it provides only empty calories— taste without the benefit of nutrition. This, in a nutshell, is what's wrong with sugar: it's not bad for you, but it's not good for you either.

by Benjamin Radford

What Is a Stroke?

 sk someone this question and you're liable to get an answer such as, "Well, you know, it's that thing that leaves people partially paralyzed." But many people don't actually know what causes a stroke or even where in the body it occurs.

A stroke can be any one of three significantly different problems with blood supply to the brain. In thrombosis, a clot builds up on a brain artery wall, cutting off blood supply and causing tissue in parts of the brain to die. An embolism is when a clot sweeps into a brain artery and clogs it, and a hemorrhage is a ruptured blood vessel in the brain, according to the American Medical Association.

Given these varying causes, and the fact that a stroke can occur in any part of the brain, symptoms can develop suddenly or over days, and outcomes vary dramatically, from headache and dizziness to paralysis or death. Stroke is the third leading cause of death in the United States.

> RISK FACTORS FOR STROKE INCLUDE SMOKING, DRINKING, LACK OF EXERCISE AND A FAMILY HISTORY OF STROKES. HIGH BLOOD PRESSURE AND HIGH CHOLESTEROL ARE BOTH PREDICTORS OF STROKES, AS ARE OBESITY AND DIABETES.

Risk factors for stroke include smoking, drinking, lack of exercise and a family history of strokes. High blood pressure and high cholesterol are both predictors of strokes, as are obesity and diabetes.

Advice from the U.S. Centers for Disease Control and Prevention: "Knowing the symptoms of a stroke, calling 911 right away, and getting to a hospital are crucial to the most beneficial outcomes after having a stroke. The best treatment is to try to prevent a stroke by taking steps to lower your risk for stroke."

> THE THREE TYPES OF STROKES WITH THEIR RATE OF OCCURRENCE.
> THROMBOSIS 40~50%   EMBOLISM 30~35%
> HEMORRHAGE 20~25%

by Robert Roy Britt

Why Do We See in 3-D?

hen it comes to seeing in 3-D, two eyes are better than one. To see how 3-D vision works, hold a finger at arm's length and look at it through one eye, then through the other. See how the image seems to jump? That's because of binocular disparity, the slight difference between the images seen by each eye.

Binocular disparity is one of the most important pieces of information the visual centers of the brain use to reconstruct the depth of a scene. If the object you're trying to view is close to you, the brain uses another clue: convergence, or the angle of your eyes as you focus on an object. Crossing your eyes will give you an extreme example of the convergence sensation.

But even without binocular vision, it's possible to judge depth. Animals without overlapping visual fields rely heavily on something called parallax, which is the difference in speed at which closer and farther objects seem to move as you pass them. For example, fence posts along the side of a highway will fly by, while a grain silo a quarter-mile from the road will seem to creep. Our brain has a built-in processing center for this phenomenon, according to a 2008 *Nature* study. An area behind the ear called the middle temporal region carries information about parallax, and may synthesize it with other depth cues.

> WE SEE IN 3-D BECAUSE OF BINOCULAR DISPARITY, THE SLIGHT DIFFERENCE BETWEEN THE IMAGES SEEN BY EACH EYE.

Other means of perceiving depth using just one eye involve cues including object size, parallel lines that appear to converge, sharper textures in closer objects, and the way objects overlap.

Even with all these cues at its disposal, the brain makes mistakes. Artists can trick the brain into seeing a 2-D painting in three dimensions by drawing converging parallel lines and painting "closer" objects in greater detail.

HOLD A FINGER AT ARM'S LENGTH AND LOOK AT IT THROUGH ONE EYE, THEN THROUGH THE OTHER. SEE HOW THE IMAGE SEEMS TO JUMP?

Gym class can be a bummer for the visual system, as well: According to a study in *Proceedings of the National Academy of Sciences*, our brains take shortcuts based on previous experience when judging depth. Because most objects we encounter move relatively slowly, we may misjudge the distance of fast-moving objects—like a soccer ball headed for your face.

by Stephanie Pappas

Chapter 2
Creatures

In a word, creatures are fascinating. There are big ones and small ones, scaly ones and fury ones. Some are soft and cuddly while others sport ferocious teeth or deadly stingers. In this chapter, we answer questions about animals and insects from all over the world which live in a variety of habitats.

What Is the Difference Between Alligators and Crocodiles?

 oming face to face with a crocodile or an alligator, you'd likely see a mouth full of serrated teeth that would scare the bejeezus out of you.

Upon closer inspection (although not recommended out in the wild) you'd spot glaring differences.

> Alligators and crocodiles look similar but do have distinct physical differences. They also live in different habitats.

The two reptile groups are close relatives, so their physical similarities are expected. They both belong to the subgroup Eusuchia, which includes about 22 species divided into three families: the fish-eating gavials or gharials, which belong to the Gavialidae; today's crocodiles or the Crocodylidae; and the Alligatoridae, or alligators. Eusuchians appeared on the scene during the late Cretaceous period some 100 million years ago.

by Jeanna Bryner

TOOTHY GRIN: When their snouts are shut, crocodiles look like they're flashing a toothy grin, as the fourth tooth on each side of the lower jaw sticks up over the upper lip. For alligators, the upper jaw is wider than the lower one, so when they close their mouths, all their teeth are hidden.

HOME BASE: Crocodiles tend to live in saltwater habitats, while alligators hang out in freshwater marshes and lakes.

SNOUT SHAPE: Alligators have wider, U-shaped snouts, while crocodiles' front ends are more pointed and V-shaped.

Why Do Cats Land on Their Feet?

 ats make it look so easy: leaping or falling from a high shelf or piece of furniture only to land gracefully on all four feet. But there's complicated feline effort that goes into falling with such style.

Cats have a highly-tuned sense of balance and have very flexible backbones (because they have more vertebrae than humans), which allows them to twist their bodies around to right themselves when they fall—an innate ability known as their "righting reflex."

When a cat jumps or falls from a high place, it uses either its sight or its vestibular apparatus (a balance system located in the inner ear) to determine up from down, and then rotates its upper body to face downward. Its lower body follows suit.

Even kittens can fall without fear, as most learn to master the skill by the time they're just seven weeks old.

Cats are also helped in falls by their small bodies, light bone structure and thick fur, which decrease their terminal velocity, thus softening the impact. Some cats will also "flatten" out their bodies, in parachute fashion, to create more resistance to air to make them fall more slowly.

> CATS HAVE WHAT'S CALLED A RIGHTING REFLEX, A HIGHLY-TUNED SENSE OF BALANCE WHICH ALLOWS THEM TO TWIST THEIR BODIES AROUND TO RIGHT THEMSELVES WHEN THEY FALL. THEY ALSO HAVE MORE VERTEBRAE THAN HUMANS, WHICH MAKES THEIR BACKS MORE FLEXIBLE.

If you have a cat, be careful about opening windows though, as a bird or squirrel can easily distract a cat enough to cause them to lose their balance—cats can still be injured in a fall, even if they do land on their feet.

Shorter falls, from one or two stories, can be riskier than higher falls because the cat may not have time to right itself.

by Life's Little Mysteries *Staff*

Can a Goldfish Really Grow to 30 Pounds?

 oung children everywhere now have a new image to fuel their nightmares about what happens to their pet goldfish after it gets flushed down the toilet. A photo of an alleged 30-pound, bright orange carp, caught by a French fisherman, has surfaced—to much speculation.

The fish in the photo actually appears to be a *Cyprinus carpio,* usually called common carp or koi, which is distinguishable by the two short whiskers called barbels surrounding its mouth and by the large scales covering its body, according to the New York Department of Environmental Conservation (DEC). The fish also has dorsal (back) and anal (bottom rear) fins, as well as a single thick fin running down its spine.

The fisherman in the photo, Raphael Biagini, reportedly claims the carp he caught and posed with for a photo (before setting it free back into the water) weighed about 30 pounds (13 kg). Biagini caught the mega fish at a lake in southern France.

It seems a carp could really weigh that much. The world's largest carp on record

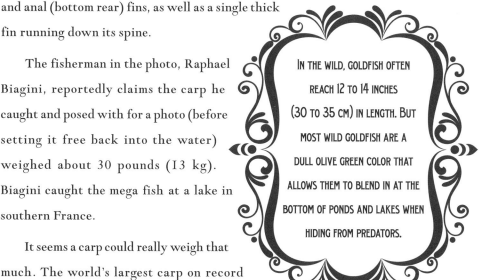

IN THE WILD, GOLDFISH OFTEN REACH 12 TO 14 INCHES (30 TO 35 CM) IN LENGTH. BUT MOST WILD GOLDFISH ARE A DULL OLIVE GREEN COLOR THAT ALLOWS THEM TO BLEND IN AT THE BOTTOM OF PONDS AND LAKES WHEN HIDING FROM PREDATORS.

weighed in at 94 pounds (42 kg) and was caught in 2010 in Rainbow Lake near Bordeaux, France, according to *The Daily Telegraph*, a UK newspaper.

A previous record-holding carp, which weighed 88 pounds (40 kg), was caught in Rainbow Lake in 2007. The fisherman named his catch Kylie after the popular Australian singer Kylie Minogue.

While it seems record-breaking carp come from France, New York's carp can grow to weigh more than 40 pounds (18 kg), according to the DEC. The largest carp found in New York waters weighed in at 50 pounds, 4 ounces (22 kg).

Goldfish *(Carassius auratus auratus)* are part of the carp family but do not have barbells around their mouths. They vary in their fin configuration, coloration and in their body size, which is directly influenced by their environment.

When they are kept as pets in small fish tanks and aquariums, goldfish tend to stay about 1-2 inches long and never grow larger than 6 inches (15 centimeters), according to the DEC.

OUI—COMMON CARP THAT LIVE IN FRENCH WATER BODIES RESEMBLE GOLDFISH, EXCEPT THEY CAN GROW TO BE MUCH, MUCH BIGGER. GOLDFISH ARE FROM THE SAME FAMILY AS CARP, COMPLETE WITH LARGE SCALES AND PUCKERED MOUTHS. HOWEVER, COMMON CARP HAVE TWO SHORT WHISKERS CALLED BARBELLS.

However, in the wild, goldfish often reach 12 to 14 inches (30 to 35 cm) in length.

Although pet goldfish are usually amber-hued or white with scarlet spots, most wild goldfish are a dull olive green color that allows them to blend in at the bottom of ponds and lakes when hiding from predators.

The title of largest pet goldfish goes to Goldie, who was 15 inches (38 cm) long, 5 inches (12 cm) wide, and weighed over 2 pounds (0.9 kg) in 2008, according to the BBC. Goldie's owner told the BBC that the fish was only an inch long when she bought it for 99 cents, and 15 years later it had ballooned into a record-breaking size, despite being kept in a small tank.

by Remy Melina

Why Don't Antarctic Fish Freeze?

The frigid waters of the Antarctic Ocean should be cold enough to freeze fish blood. A natural antifreeze, however, keeps the fish blood flowing.

The Antarctic Ocean's freezing temperatures of 28.8°F (minus 1.8°C) are lower than the freezing point of fish blood, which is about 30.4°F (minus 0.9°C), which would seem to suggest that all those fish should be frozen in their tracks.

How fish are able to keep moving at these temperatures puzzled researchers for more than 50 years until special frost protection proteins were found in the blood of cold-water fish. These so-called antifreeze proteins work better than any household antifreeze at keeping the fish from becoming fish-cicles. How they work, however, has been unclear.

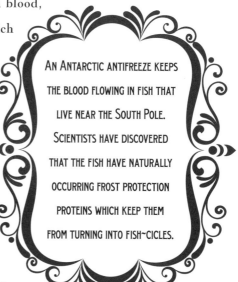

AN ANTARCTIC ANTIFREEZE KEEPS THE BLOOD FLOWING IN FISH THAT LIVE NEAR THE SOUTH POLE. SCIENTISTS HAVE DISCOVERED THAT THE FISH HAVE NATURALLY OCCURRING FROST PROTECTION PROTEINS WHICH KEEP THEM FROM TURNING INTO FISH~CICLES.

To get to the bottom of this chemical question, scientists studied the antifreeze proteins of the Antarctic toothfish *(Dissostichus mawsoni)*, which one of the researchers caught while on an Antarctic expedition.

Scientists used a special technique to record the motion of water molecules mixed with antifreeze proteins from the fish. In the presence of these antifreeze proteins, the water molecules danced a more ordered dance than they otherwise would have. In other words, the antifreeze proteins disturbed the water molecules in such a way that they could not bond together and form ice crystals.

"The disco dance becomes a minuet," says study team member Martina Havenith of the Ruhr University Bochum in Germany. The study was detailed in the *Journal of the American Chemical Society*.

by Life's Little Mysteries *Staff*

Why Don't Woodpeckers Get Headaches?

Woodpeckers hit their heads up to 20 times a second. But muscles, bones and an extra eyelid protect their small bird brains.

Strong, dense muscles in the bird's neck give it strength to repeatedly thump its head. But it is extra muscles in the skull that keep the bird from getting hurt. These muscles act like a protective helmet for the brain.

Unlike the human brain, the woodpecker's brain is tightly confined by muscles in the skull and

COMPRESSIBLE SKULL BONES AND EXTRA MUSCLES IN THEIR HEADS KEEP WOOD-PECKERS FROM GETTING HURT. TOGETHER, THESE SPECIAL FEATURES ACT LIKE A PROTECTIVE HELMET.

a compressible bone. This keeps a woodpecker's brain from jiggling around when the bird is stabbing away at a tree trunk.

A millisecond before making impact, a woodpecker contracts its neck muscles. Then, it closes its thick inner eyelid. The eyelid acts like a seat belt for the eye, says University of California Davis ophthalmologist Ivan Schwab, whose 2007 study on this phenomenon was published in the *British Journal of Ophthalmology*. Without an extra eyelid, the retina could tear, and worse, the eye could pop out of its socket.

TO PROTECT ITS EYES, A WOODPECKER HAS AN EXTRA EYELID THAT CLOSES A MILLISECOND BEFORE IT STARTS ITS UNIQUE, MINI-JACKHAMMER BEHAVIOR ON THE SIDES OF TREE TRUNKS.

These safeguards are especially important to males, which peck up to 12,000 times a day during courtship.

No matter the occasion, a woodpecker will only make straight strikes to a tree. The birds prevent head trauma by not making any side-to-side movements.

by Corey Binns

What Makes Fireflies Light Up?

The beautiful, but seemingly random, blinking patterns of fireflies have been decoded. Turns out, it's all about love.

Scientists have been attempting to understand the purpose of large groups of fireflies' mysterious synchronized flashes since the 1930s. A new experiment, the first ever to create a virtual environment for fireflies—using LED lights as artificial males—has revealed how the female firefly's nervous system processes visual signals, as well as the role that male flash synchrony, or timing of the lighting, plays in the responsiveness of the female.

Fireflies use bioluminescence, or naturally occurring chemical glow, for sexual selection. They synchronize the flashing of their neon-green lights in large groups in order to help female fireflies recognize potential mates, according to the findings.

FIREFLIES USE THEIR BIOLUMINESCENCE WHEN SELECTING A MATE. AS A FORM OF MORSE CODE, BOTH GENDERS OF THE INSECT SEND OUT NEON~GREEN SIGNALS TO HELP FEMALES RECOGNIZE POTENTIAL MATES.

"There have been lots of really good observations and hypotheses about firefly synchrony," says lead author Andrew Moiseff of the University of Connecticut. "But until now, no one has experimentally tested whether synchrony has a function."

Flashing together makes it easier for members of the species of *Photinus carolinus* fireflies to locate appropriate partners for mating, the study found. In firefly mating rituals, the males cruise by, flying around and flashing their signals to let the ladies know that they are looking for love.

Meanwhile, female fireflies wait in the leaves, observing the males' flashes. Each waits for a specific pattern of blinking light—sequences are unique to each species. When they spot a pattern that they like, they flash the same signal back at the male as an invitation to come on over.

Scientists estimate that, of the roughly 2,000 species of fireflies around the world, only about one percent synchronize their flashes in large groups. However, flashing Photinus fireflies are very common, especially in North America. They evolved to flash in synchronizing patterns as a solution to specific behavioral, environmental or physiological conditions, says Moiseff.

Also known as lightning bugs, fireflies are very goal-oriented: after living underground as larvae for about two years before emerging, Photinus fireflies spend their brief, two-week-long adult lives courting and mating. In fact, they are so dedicated to finding a mate and reproducing that they don't even stop to eat.

With literally only one thing on their minds, and in the midst of fierce competition over female attention, why do male fireflies partake in synchronized flashing in a large group?

Synchronous species of fireflies are often found in high densities, making it hard for female fireflies to see and register a lone male firefly's signal. This suggests that there is a problem in the female's information processing, which group synchronized flashing seems to compensate for, according to the study.

By flashing the same pattern simultaneously, male fireflies are sending out a clear, unified declaration of their species to the females. Using LED lights, researchers tested this hypothesis on female fireflies, noting that they responded to flashes in perfect or near perfect unison more than 80 percent of the time.

A RECENT STUDY OF THE NERVOUS SYSTEMS OF FEMALE FIREFLIES USED LED LIGHTS AS ARTIFICIAL MALES. IT REVEALED THE ROLE THAT MALE FLASH SYNCHRONY PLAYS IN THE RESPONSIVENESS OF THE FEMALE.

But once a female sees the mass synchronized signal and responds, how does she decide who in the group is to be her paramour?

"In the field, under natural conditions, we find that a responding female *Photinus carolinus* attracted several males," Moiseff tells *Life's Little Mysteries*. "These males then cluster around her and interact among each other, as well as with the female."

Researchers do not know whether the female's initial response is directed at a single male within the synchronous group, or whether she is responding nonspecifically to the group as a whole. But because her response flash attracts many males, it appears that she isn't communicating with any individual male.

"Ultimately, however, she selects a single male to mate with," Moiseff adds. "The effect of this is that female choice is occurring separately from initial species recognition and attraction."

by Remy Melina

Why Do Whales Beach Themselves?

esearchers have several theories to explain why some whales, which are expert navigators by nature, strand themselves in shallow water and on beaches. Strandings can involve a lone whale or a whole pod, and some even appear to be intentional.

The mystery is becoming an increasingly important one to solve because large pods of stranded whales are becoming more common, especially among beak nose whales.

In 2010, more than 70 beached whales came up on the coast of New Zealand, although humans were able to get some back out to sea. The event has led marine biologists to try to determine what causes the mass whale strandings.

The whales stranded in northwest Auckland are pilot whales, which are known as one of the

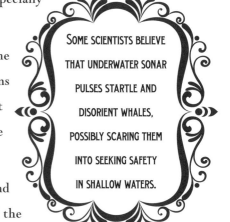

SOME SCIENTISTS BELIEVE THAT UNDERWATER SONAR PULSES STARTLE AND DISORIENT WHALES, POSSIBLY SCARING THEM INTO SEEKING SAFETY IN SHALLOW WATERS.

most common whales to beach themselves, says Scott Baker, marine biologist and professor at the Marine Mammal Institute at Oregon State University.

Some researchers and environmentalists argue that underwater sonar pulses startle and disorient whales, possibly scaring them into seeking safety in shallow waters. Beak nose and melon-headed whales may be particularly affected by the mid-frequency sonar waves that the U.S. Navy uses to detect submarines, according to the National Oceanic and Atmospheric Administration (NOAA).

A 2001 study conducted by the Bahamas Marine Animals Research Organization found a correlation between mass strandings of beak nose whales in the northern Bahamas and naval sonar maneuvers in the area.

The Natural Resources Defense Council and other environmental groups settled a lawsuit against the Navy in 2008, and the Navy agreed to further investigate how sonar technology affects whales and other marine mammals. Previous lawsuits in California and Hawaii led to the federal courts ordering the Navy to curb its use of sonar.

However, scientists have yet to determine exactly how sonar pulses disturb or harm whales, or why they affect certain species more than others.

Individual whales may beach themselves for a host of reasons. Genetic mutations, illnesses from infections or parasites, injuries from predators or entanglements in fishing gear and old age may all play a role, according to cetacean science researchers at Whitehead lab at Dalhousie University in Nova Scotia.

But the reasons behind group strandings are more mysterious. "Mass strandings are an interesting problem," Baker tells *Life's Little Mysteries*. "The cause of a group stranding is often hard to determine because it is difficult to study the behavior of whales pre-stranding."

One hypothesis is that a pod of whales may accidentally strand themselves when attempting to come to the aid of a beached whale that is sending out distress calls. However, because most stranded whales are in poor shape by the time marine-life rescuers reach them, it's hard to determine if only one whale was originally in danger, Baker says.

Nutrient deficiencies, disorientation and weakness brought on by a lack of food at whales' feeding grounds may bring whales into shallow waters. They may follow prey (or be attempting to escape predators) into shallow waters, according to Whitehead Lab.

Rough weather, water pollution (such as oil spills) and environmental toxins are other possible causes put forth by researchers. Poisonous red tides, which occur when microscopic algae rapidly bloom and release toxins, not only affect whales but also filter-feeding shellfish and other parts of the marine food chain, according to NOAA.

OTHER SCIENTISTS BELIEVE THAT NUTRIENT DEFICIENCIES, DISORIENTATION AND WEAKNESS BROUGHT ON BY A LACK OF FOOD AT WHALES' FEEDING GROUNDS MAY CAUSE THEM TO BEACH. THEY MAY FOLLOW PREY (OR BE ATTEMPTING TO ESCAPE PREDATORS) INTO SHALLOW WATERS.

Another theory is based on the social bonds and kinship within a pod. Most whale species travel in groups as a survival strategy, with dominant whales leading the pod. If the dominant whale becomes sick or confused, it may lead the pod too close to shore, where they can become trapped by a low tide, according to *Whales*, a book published by Capstone Press.

The largest reported stranding of a single whale species occurred in 1946, when 835 false killer whales stranded themselves near the city of Mar del Plata in Argentina, according to the *Encyclopedia of Marine Mammals*. The cause of the massive beaching was never determined.

"There are lots of reasons for group strandings, but no agreements," Baker says.

by Remy Melina

What Is the Longest-Living Animal?

he animal with the most birthdays to date goes to a quahog clam plucked from the cold Icelandic waters in 2007. The tiny mollusk would need quite a lung capacity to extinguish the possible 400 candles on its cake.

On average, members of the quahog clan don't live nearly as long. When talking about the longest and shortest life spans, scientists refer to the average age at which an organism is expected to die. Maximum life spans highlight those individuals whose ages "break the molds."

The Galápagos tortoise has an average life span of more than 150 years. They certainly take advantage of their lengthy lives, ambling around at a sluggish 0.16 miles per hour (0.26 kph).

by Life's Little Mysteries *Staff*

Some life-span chart toppers include:
- American box turtle 120 years
- Bowhead whale 60 to 70 years (though they can exceed 200 years)
- Elephant 70 years
- Human 70 to 80 years

Some animals are born and die in the seeming blink of the eye, including:
- Adult housefly 4 weeks
- Worker bee 5 weeks
- Ant (Worker) 1/2 year
- Opossum 1 year
- Ant (Queen) 3 years
- Rat 2-3 years

What Are Dog Years?

ogs age more quickly than humans, and, as many of us can attest, they sadly don't stick around for the entire life of their owners. The "dog year" measure is an attempt to quantify this difference in life spans—to give an age to our furry pets as if they were to live as long as humans.

The most common system for calculating a pet's age in dog years is to multiply it by seven. The age of a 1-year-old Miniature Poodle in dog years would be 7 and that of a 2-year-old Great Dane would be 14. This system assumes the average lifespan of humans to be 70 years and for dogs, 10 years.

Using this multiplier, however, has several flaws, says Stanley Coren, professor at the University of British Columbia who has written many books on dogs. For starters, 70 years is no longer the average lifespan of humans, and a dog's lifespan varies depending on its size and breed. The fatal flaw is that at 1 year, dogs are able to reproduce puppies. This is not the case for a 7-year-old child.

> THEY MAY BE A MAN'S BEST FRIEND, BUT UNFORTUNATELY, DOGS DON'T LIVE AS LONG AS HUMANS. HOWEVER, THE STANDARD SEVEN-YEAR MULTIPLIER TO ESTIMATE HOW A DOG'S AGE COMPARES TO A HUMAN'S HAS FLAWS.

Coren has come up with his own way to calculate a dog's age in human terms. In his system, a 1-year-old dog is like a 16-year-old person; at 2 the dog is like a 24-year-old person; and for the next three years until the dog reaches the age of 5, each year adds five human years.

Beyond age 5, the dog's size must be accounted for in the equation, Coren says. Typically, small dogs live longer than large ones. To account for this difference, Coren suggests adding four years of human life to the age of small dogs after age 5, and six years for large breeds.

Using Coren's system, a 1-year-old Miniature Poodle would be 16 dog years and the much larger, 2-year-old Great Dane would be 24 dog years. When each pup has graced the Earth for eight "real" years, the Miniature Poodle would be 51 dog years, and the Great Dane would be 54.

by Michelle Bryner

How Do Lizards Cool Off?

eptiles use the environment to regulate their warmth. This strategy helps them conserve energy in the cold and rapidly ramp up their body temperature in the heat, but it also makes them particularly sensitive to climate change.

For most lizards and snakes, cooling down is as easy as moving into the shade or hiding under a rock, says Jack Conrad, a research associate at the American Museum of Natural History in New York and a specialist in reptile biology. Reptiles warm up just as simply—by basking in the sun.

> As cold-blooded animals, reptiles such as lizards depend on the environment to regulate their body temperature. Cooling down from the hot sun means sitting in the shade.

"If you have a lizard in a desert that feels like it needs to warm up for its metabolism to work better, it goes and sits on a rock in the sun," Conrad tells *Life's Little Mysteries*. "If it gets too warm from running around, it goes and sits under a rock in the shade."

However, some very large and very small reptiles regulate their temperature a bit differently. Very big lizards like the Komodo dragon have so much mass that their bodies trap a lot of heat, allowing them to maintain a fairly consistent body temperature, almost like a mammal.

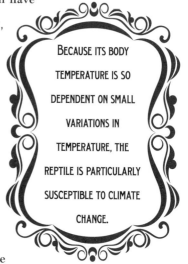

BECAUSE ITS BODY TEMPERATURE IS SO DEPENDENT ON SMALL VARIATIONS IN TEMPERATURE, THE REPTILE IS PARTICULARLY SUSCEPTIBLE TO CLIMATE CHANGE.

But for small lizards, maintaining this consistency is more difficult. Their bodies cool down and heat up when the air around them changes temperature even slightly. Small lizards can feel changes as subtle as the sun moving behind a cloud, and their metabolisms slow down to a level near that of hibernation when they rest in the shade. Then, when they move into the sunlight, the lizards become hyperactive.

Because they draw heat from the environment, instead of relying on the complicated internal mechanisms that mammals have to regulate their temperature, lizards can survive on far less food than mammals. In fact, some reptiles can go an entire year between meals thanks to this strategy.

But a life so dependent on small variations in temperature also makes climate change particularly dangerous for reptiles.

"Even 30 years ago, when people were just beginning to detect something going on with the climate, one of the first groups they looked at was forest lizards," Conrad says. "If the climate change is dramatic, you will see a lot of diversity go away. There are about 9,000 lizards and snakes living today, and you will see that number drop dramatically."

by Stuart Fox

How Big Were Baby Dinosaurs?

inosaurs came in many shapes and sizes, and so did their babies. The smallest eggs found were just a few centimeters long. One chicken-sized dinosaur, Sinosauropteryx, was found fossilized with unlaid eggs in her abdomen, researchers reported in 1998 in the journal *Nature*. The eggs were about 1.5 inches (4 cm) long and just over 1 inch (2.5 cm) wide, which is a little smaller than a chicken egg.

> EVEN LARGE DINOSAURS HAD SMALL BABIES. BABY DINOSAURS RANGED FROM ABOUT 6 INCHES TO 3 FEET AT THE TIME OF HATCHING.

But even large dinosaurs had small babies. In a 2005 *Science* paper, researchers reported the discovery of an embryo that was 6 inches (15 cm) long, curled in an egg just 2.5 inches (6 cm) long. The species was Massospondylus, a plant-eater with an adult length of about 16 feet (5 m).

Maiasaurus, the "good mother lizard," was as long as a school bus when grown, but only 1 foot (30 cm) long when coming out of its egg. And the long-necked Camarasaurus grew from a hatchling 3 feet (1 m) long to a behemoth with a length of 59 feet (18 m).

To attain their huge bulk, these prehistoric giants had some impressive growth spurts. Using data from growth plates in bones, researchers estimated that to reach an adult weight of 57,094 pounds (25,952 kg), a baby Apatosaurus would pack on more than 30 pounds (14 kg) per day—about the same rate as modern whales, according to the Journal *Nature*.

That might seem like a lot, but when your largest predator is the toothy, 17-foot-tall Allosaurus, there's no lack of motivation to get big and strong.

by Stephanie Pappas

What Is it Like to Be an Ant?

Hungry? Pull up to the nearest ant in your colony and open wide—the other ant will regurgitate a drop of liquid.

Food is truly communal in this co-op, for once a morsel is introduced into your colony, before long it will be in the bellies of nearly every ant in the nest. In addition to your social stomach, you ants also seem to have a collective brain. Your sense of awareness is severely limited in comparison to the higher-level processing of the human mind. You are capable of learning and making choices (perhaps a sign of rudimentary free will), but your actions are largely controlled by chemical secretions from other ants in the colony.

Far from any monarchal might, it is a queen ant's odor that orders other ants to their apportioned tasks.

by Ben Mauk

LIKE THE BORG RACE IN THE MOVIE *STAR TREK: FIRST CONTACT*, ANTS' COMMUNAL EXISTENCE ACTUALLY SHARES A COLLECTIVE INTELLIGENCE. THEIR ACTIONS ARE LARGELY CONTROLLED BY CHEMICAL SECRETIONS FROM FELLOW ANTS IN A COLONY.

How Do Oysters Make Pearls?

 natural pearl begins its life inside an oyster's shell when an intruder, such as a grain of sand or bit of floating food, slips in between the shells of the oyster, a type of mollusk, and the protective layer that covers the mollusk's organs, called the mantle.

In order to protect itself from irritation, the oyster will quickly begin covering the uninvited visitor with layers of nacre— the mineral substance that fashions the mollusk's shells. Layer upon layer of nacre, also known as mother-of-pearl, coat the grain of sand until the iridescent gem is formed.

Cultured pearls are made in the same way. The only difference is that instead of accidental circumstances beginning the process, a "pearl farmer" embeds a grain of sand into the mollusk.

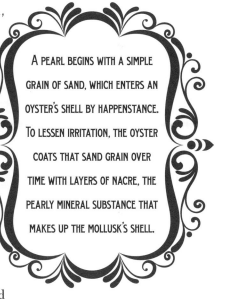

A PEARL BEGINS WITH A SIMPLE GRAIN OF SAND, WHICH ENTERS AN OYSTER'S SHELL BY HAPPENSTANCE. TO LESSEN IRRITATION, THE OYSTER COATS THAT SAND GRAIN OVER TIME WITH LAYERS OF NACRE, THE PEARLY MINERAL SUBSTANCE THAT MAKES UP THE MOLLUSK'S SHELL.

by Michelle Bryner

Chapter 3
Culture

The United States is a diverse community rich with culture
and identity. In this chapter, we provide answers about
American customs, holiday traditions and historical
conventions that affect us every day.

What's the History of the Barbecue?

A favorite American pastime and a summer tradition for many, barbecues have a long and surprisingly patriotic history.

They began when a human ancestor called *Homo erectus* began cooking meat with fire about 1.8 million years ago, says Steven Raichlen in his book *Planet Barbecue*. But barbecuing the way that Americans know it now—meat cooked on an outdoor grill or pit and covered in spices and basting sauce—originated in the Caribbean.

The word "barbecue" comes from the language of a Caribbean Indian tribe called the Taino. Their word for grilling on a raised wooden grate is "barbacoa." The word first appeared in print in a Spanish explorer's account of the West Indies in 1526.

> THE WORD "BARBECUE" COMES FROM THE WORD "BARBACOA," FROM THE LANGUAGE OF A CARIBBEAN INDIAN TRIBE CALLED THE TAINO. THE WORD DESCRIBES GRILLING ON A RAISED WOODEN GRATE. "BARBACOA" FIRST APPEARED IN PRINT IN A SPANISH EXPLORER'S ACCOUNT OF THE WEST INDIES IN 1526.

Since then, the popularity of barbecues has spread like wildfire. The history of barbecuing in America dates to colonial times, and it has been a part of American culture ever since. In fact, one of the first laws enacted in the colony of Virginia during the 1650s forbade the discharge of guns at a barbecue.

"When we won the Revolutionary War, laid the cornerstone of the Capitol, and built the first bridge over the Missouri River, the events were commemorated with barbecues," says Raichlen, who is also the host of *Primal Grill* on PBS.

Our presidents were known to be big fans of the laid-back pastime as well. George Washington's diaries abound with references to barbecues, including one that lasted for three days.

THE WEDDING FEAST OF ABRAHAM LINCOLN'S PARENTS WAS A BARBEQUE.

"George Washington was a major barbecue buff," Raichlen tells *Life's Little Mysteries*. "When Abraham Lincoln's parents were married, their wedding feast was a barbecue."

Along the way, famous inventors left their mark on the American barbecue: The first commercial charcoal briquette factory was designed by Thomas Edison and built by Henry Ford in 1921.

Today, barbecuing plays an especially large role in Southern cuisine, which is notorious for its rich and zesty flavor. For example, the people of Owensboro, Ky., have been barbecuing mutton—not delicate lamb, but big, gamey mutton—for more than 150 years. It's still a specialty in the town, where it's served with the world's only black barbecue sauce.

by Remy Melina

When Does Ramadan Begin?

amadan is the holiest month on the Islamic calendar because it was during this month that Muslims believe their holy book, the Koran, was first revealed by Allah to the prophet Muhammad.

Because Islamic holidays are tied to a lunar calendar, the exact times for the beginning and end of Ramadan are not known in advance each year. In 2010, Ramadan began on Aug. 11 and concluded on Sept. 10.

In *The Religious World*, Islamic scholar Azim Nanji describes Ramadan. "Fasting begins at daybreak and ends after the setting of the sun. The spiritual, moral and physical discipline observed during these hours include a more intensive commitment to the values and practices of Islam, as well as refraining from food, drink, and sexual activity. ... The rhythm of abstinence and quietude during the daylight hours of Ramadan alternates with times of feasting and socializing throughout the evenings."

> "FASTING BEGINS AT DAYBREAK AND ENDS AFTER THE SUN SETS," SAYS AZIM NANJI IN THE RELIGIOUS WORLD ABOUT RAMADAN. "THE SPIRITUAL, MORAL AND PHYSICAL DISCIPLINE OBSERVED DURING THESE HOURS INCLUDE A MORE INTENSIVE COMMITMENT TO THE VALUES AND PRACTICES OF ISLAM."

Fasting is one of the five pillars, or main duties, required of all able-bodied Muslims. The other pillars are daily prayer, making a pilgrimage to Mecca at least once in a lifetime, charity, and making a profession of faith.

by Benjamin Radford

Why Do We Dress Up on Halloween?

very year, kids—and sometimes adults—dress up in ridiculous outfits and storm the streets, on a mission to ring strangers' doorbells and fill bags with candy. As kids, we accept trick o' treating as normal behavior, but the October 31 tradition is really quite strange when you think about it.

The traditions and folklore of Halloween are a hybrid of Pagan, Celtic, Catholic and ancient Roman traditions. The holiday is thought to date to the Iron Age (around 800-600 BC), when the Celts and Gauls ruled parts of Great Britain and northern France. October 31 marks the last day of the Celtic calendar, and for Celtic-folklore believers, Halloween was a day of celebration before winter, which brought the harvest and the death of life and nature.

HALLOWEEN LIKELY BEGAN AROUND 800-600 BC WHEN THE CELTS AND GAULS RULED PARTS OF GREAT BRITAIN AND NORTHERN FRANCE.

Similarly, Gaelic people believed it was important to honor the dead on what was, essentially, their New Year's celebration. They called the holiday Samhain, or the "summer's end" in Old Irish, according to *Halloween: From Pagan Ritual to Party Night*.

When the Romans invaded Gaul (modern day France) and Britain in first century BC, many of their festival traditions became mixed with those of Samhain. In particular, the ancient Roman festival of Pomona, the Roman goddess of fruits and gardens, was held around Nov. 1, and it celebrated the apple harvest. Scholars say traditions from the darker Roman festivals of the dead called Parentalia and Feralia, although held in February, were also incorporated as Halloween celebrations spread throughout Europe.

In the Roman Catholic Church, All Saints' Day, which is also referred to as All Hallows or Hallowmas, is celebrated on Nov. 1 and is a day for honoring saints and the recently departed.

The traditions came to include practices to ward off spirits and to honor the dead in European countries. The British believed fire warded off evil spirits, so churches bought extra candles and held bonfires in graveyards. The Spanish visited graveyards and consecrated graves with holy water or milk. French monks took a less superstitious action on the day, sending prayers to saints, according to *Halloween: From Pagan Ritual to Party Night*.

The Irish, however, were really the first to start the tradition of trick o' treating. Halloween reached America in the mid-19th century with the influx of Irish immigrants who brought their mix of Samhain, Pomona and pagan traditions.

Although the holiday clearly is derived from the Church, Halloween has always been a sensitive subject in terms of religion. Some have argued Halloween is a ritual for devil worship and have tried to find evidence of animal or human sacrifice in ancient traditions associated with the holiday. However, the Christian Coalition declared in 1982 that Hallowmas or Samhain were not "satanic rituals."

Today, the holiday has influence on many different countries around the world. Because of the French Catholic Church's strong campaign against Halloween, the French did not celebrate the holiday until the mid-1990s, but today, for their "La Fête d'Halloween," people go from store to store collecting candy, not from house to house. Children will sometimes ask for flowers or money to decorate tombstones.

Germans celebrate, or rather protect themselves, from Halloween by hiding all the knives in their houses in case spirits with old grudges return to cause trouble.

Swedish students get a full week off for Halloween, or what they call "Alla Helgons," and adults have shorter workdays.

Of course, many countries with a strong Catholic influence, such as Mexico, celebrate the holiday closer to how the ancients did, with visits to cemeteries to bless the graves and to send prayers, according to *The Halloween Handbook*.

by Lily Norton

Who Started Daylight Saving Time?

Daylight saving time, a source of confusion and mystery for many, usually ends on the first Sunday of November each year. The idea of resetting clocks forward an hour in the spring and back an hour in the fall was first suggested by Benjamin Franklin in his essay, "An Economical Project for Diminishing the Cost of Light," which was published in the *Journal de Paris* in April 1784.

Franklin's suggestion was largely overlooked until it was brought up again in 1907 by Englishman William Willett, who penned a pamphlet called "The Waste of Daylight." Although the British House of Commons rejected Willett's proposal to advance the clock one hour in the spring and back again in autumn in 1908, British Summer Time was introduced by the Parliament in 1916.

> BENJAMIN FRANKLIN FIRST SUGGESTED THE IDEA OF RESETTING CLOCKS FORWARD AN HOUR IN THE SPRING AND BACK AN HOUR IN THE FALL, BUT THE PRACTICE WASN'T INSTITUTED IN THE UNITED STATES UNTIL 1918.

Many other countries change their clocks when adjusting to summertime, but the United States only began doing so towards the end of World War I in an attempt to conserve energy. The House of Representatives voted 252 to 40 to pass a law "to save daylight," with the official first daylight saving time taking place on March 15, 1918. The occasion was initially met with much resistance, says Michael Downing in his book *Spring Forward: The Annual Madness of Daylight Saving Time.*

"When Congress poked its finger into the face of every clock in the country, millions of Americans winced," Downing writes. "United by a determination to beat back the

ORIGINALLY, CLOCKS WERE SPRUNG FORWARD ON THE LAST SUNDAY IN APRIL AND TURNED BACK ON THE LAST SUNDAY IN OCTOBER, BUT THE ENERGY POLICY ACT OF 2005 SHIFTED THE PERIOD OF DAYLIGHT SAVING TIME TO OCCUR FROM THE SECOND SUNDAY IN MARCH TO THE FIRST SUNDAY IN NOVEMBER.

big hand of government," daylight saving time opponents "raised holy hell, vowing to return the nation to real time, normal time, farm time, sun time—the time they liked to think of as 'God's time.'"

Despite the public outcry, government officials enforced the time change until 1919, when they allowed state and local governments to decide whether to continue the practice. It was reinstituted during World War II but after the war the decision again fell to the states.

In fact, even when Congress officially made the time change a law under the Uniform Time Act of 1966, it only stated that if the public decided to observe daylight saving time, it must do so uniformly. Hawaii and Arizona (with the exception of the Navajo Reservation), still choose not to partake in the convention, as do some U.S. territories, including American Samoa, Guam, Puerto Rico and the Virgin Islands.

Originally, clocks were sprung forward on the last Sunday in April and turned back on the last Sunday in October, but the Energy Policy Act of 2005 shifted the period of daylight saving time to occur from the second Sunday in March to the first Sunday in November.

by Remy Melina

Why Are Men's and Women's Buttons on Opposite Sides?

It seems a little odd—and it's not something that anyone but costumers, cross-dressers, and tailors have occasion to notice much—but men's shirts and women's blouses button from different directions.

This might make sense if most women were left-handed and most men were right-handed, but as it is, most people are right-handed. So what's the deal?

The reason has its roots in both custom and fashion. In the last few centuries of modern dress, both men and women wore more clothes than they do today (which is probably just as well, as they also bathed a lot less than they do today).

Depending on the era, men might wear waistcoats, pantaloons, gaiters and wool jackets. But women's clothing was far more elaborate, and could consist of a dozen or more garments including petticoats, bloomers, gowns, corsets and bustles.

WOMEN'S BUTTONS WERE PLACED IN THE OPPOSITE DIRECTION OF MEN'S BUTTONS FOR CONVENIENCE. UNTIL MODERN TIMES, NOBLE WOMEN, WHO WORE MORE LAYERS OF CLOTHING THAN MEN, WERE DRESSED BY MAIDSERVANTS. DESPITE THE DRASTIC CHANGE IN MODERN CUSTOMS, THE FASHION TRADITION HAS REMAINED.

Thus, especially in middle- and upper-class society, men generally dressed themselves, whereas women did not. Instead, maidservants might spend an hour or more dressing the lady of the house. Clothiers soon realized that reversing the buttons on women's clothes made the job faster and easier for all involved. Because men were not dressed by servants, there was no need to reverse the buttons on their garments, and thus a custom was born.

Why has this tradition carried into the modern era, when women can dress themselves, thank you very much? For the same reason that most people still type on the QWERTY keyboard: it's customary. There's no real reason the buttons couldn't be switched—it's just that nobody has bothered to change a tradition that few people notice or complain about in the first place.

by Benjamin Radford

What's the Difference Between a Duchess and a Princess?

hile both duchesses and princesses are royalty, and princesses technically outrank duchesses, the relationship between the two titles is not always clearly defined. And sometimes, a princess isn't really a princess at all. We'll explain.

Princesses are usually the daughters or granddaughters of a king or queen. Traditionally, a "commoner," or a woman possessing no royal rank, can gain the title of princess by marrying a prince, with the possibility of later becoming a queen.

A duchess, on the other hand, is the wife or widow of a duke, or a woman who equally holds the rank of duke in her own right, says John C. Francis in *The Index to Main Families, Persons, Places and Subjects in Egle's Notes and Queries.*

In European nobility, the duke is the highest rank below the monarch, or king. The title of duke was first introduced by ancient Romans, who used it to describe tribal Germanic and Celtic war leaders, according to *A History of England Before the Norman Conquest.* During the Middle Ages, dukes ruled over provinces and were the highest-ranking peers of the king in feudal monarchies.

A princess or queen can also have the title of duchess and vice versa, says M. Joseph in *Lords of the Land*. For example, in 1986 when Sarah Ferguson married Prince Andrew (Queen Elizabeth II's second son), she became a princess. And because Andrew also held the title of Duke of York, she became the Duchess of York.

And sometimes women can even be dukes. Queen Elizabeth II, who was a princess for 26 years before becoming the current Queen of England, also holds the titles of Duke of Normandy in the Channel Islands and Duke of Lancaster in Lancashire.

If a woman becomes a princess through marriage, she loses her royal title if the couple divorces. The same rules apply to the title of duchess.

> IT IS POSSIBLE TO BE BOTH A DUCHESS AND A PRINCESS. SARAH FERGUSON WAS A PRINCESS BECAUSE OF THE FORMAL TITLE THAT QUEEN ELIZABETH II GAVE HER, AND SHE WAS A DUCHESS BECAUSE HER HUSBAND PRINCE ANDREW HELD THE TITLE OF DUKE OF YORK. HOWEVER, SHE LOST BOTH TITLES IN 1996 WHEN THE COUPLE DIVORCED.

Princess Diana, who married Queen Elizabeth II's son, Prince Charles, in 1981 and became the Princess of Wales when she was 20 years old, famously said, "Being a princess isn't all it's cracked up to be."

And while "Disney duchess" doesn't quite have the same ring to it as "Disney princess," there have been a few duchesses in Disney film history, including the quite unpleasant Duchess character in *Alice in Wonderland* and the pedigreed mother cat from *The Aristocats*.

by Remy Melina

Why Is the Flag at Half-Staff Only Until Noon on Memorial Day?

 or 142 years, Americans have taken the last Monday in May to remember those who have died in our wars. Like all deaths honored by the state, flags fly at half-staff. However, on Memorial Day, the U.S. flag only flies at half-staff for the first half of the day, and then it is raised to full height from noon to sundown. This unique custom honors the war dead for the morning, and the living veterans for the rest of the day.

No one knows the exact date this tradition began, but an Army regulations book from 1906 carries instructions for the procedure, so it predates the 20th century, says Clark Rogers, executive director of the National Flag Foundation.

In 1924, Congress codified the tradition into U.S. Code Title 4, Section 6, with the proclamation, "For the nation lives, and the flag is a symbol of illumination," explaining how the noon flag-raising symbolizes the persistence of the nation in the face of loss, Rogers tells *Life's Little Mysteries*.

BEFORE VETERAN'S DAY WAS OBSERVED ON NOV. 11 EACH YEAR, MEMORIAL DAY WAS A HOLIDAY FOR BOTH THE WAR DEAD AND THE LIVING VETERANS WHO HAVE SERVED IN THE U.S. MILITARY.

"The first part of the day honors those who sacrificed, and the second part of the day honors those who are still with us," Rogers says.

The precise origin of a half-raised flag as a way to honor the fallen is also unclear, Rogers said. Some traditions say the lowered flag allows room for an invisible flag of death to fly above it. Others point to the tradition in naval warfare of lowering a flag to indicate surrender. There are also claims that lowering a flag symbolically recreates the ancient Greco-Roman tradition of signaling death with a broken column or staff. Currently, at least 21 countries use a lowered flag to honor the dead.

Honoring the dead, especially the war dead, played a key role in post-Civil War America, says David Blight, a professor of history at Yale University and author of *Beyond the Battlefield: Race, Memory, and the American Civil War*. Both the Union and the Confederacy began honoring lost soldiers before the war even ended, as war widows combed battlefields in search of their fallen relatives. Eventually, the flowers that mourners left at the graves across the nation merged with the May celebrations of freed slaves to form a national Memorial Day.

ON MEMORIAL DAY, THE U.S. FLAG ONLY FLIES AT HALF-STAFF FOR THE FIRST HALF OF THE DAY, AND THEN IT IS RAISED TO FULL HEIGHT FROM NOON TO SUNDOWN. THIS UNIQUE CUSTOM HONORS THE WAR DEAD FOR THE MORNING, AND THE LIVING VETERANS FOR THE REST OF THE DAY.

The celebration of this holiday, which gained an official designation on May 30, 1868, began falling out of practice in the beginning of the 20th century, but then reentered popular practice during World War I.

Then, after World War II, advocacy by veterans' groups led to the creation of a separate holiday for living military personnel in the form of Veteran's Day. Thus, Memorial Day became a day exclusively for celebrating the sacrifice of those who fell in battle, leaving only the mid-day flag-raising to signal hope beyond death.

by Stuart Fox

Where Did the Piñata Originate?

Many brightly colored piñatas are strung up to be whacked each Cinco de Mayo.

This Mexican tradition has been celebrated for hundreds of years and was brought to the New World by the Spanish. But who brought piñatas to Spain?

Though the Spanish origin of piñatas is largely undisputed among historians, some evidence also points to China as the original root of the piñata custom. And the tradition may have made a stop in Italy on the way from China to Spain.

At least as far back as the 13th century, the Chinese had a game whereby large paper dolls in animal shapes were stuffed with seeds and then smashed to bits by partygoers, according to the Center for History and New Media at George Mason University and the University of Missouri at Kansas City. The paper remnants were then burned and the ashes kept for good luck.

Explorer Marco Polo saw this game during his travels to China and brought the idea back to Italy, where the object was called a pignatta—or "little pot"—and became

THE PIÑATA ORIGINATES FROM THE JOURNEY OF ITALIAN EXPLORER MARCO POLO TO CHINA IN THE 13TH CENTURY. THE TRADITION LATER TRAVELED TO SPAIN. SPANISH MISSIONARIES TOOK IT TO MEXICO, WHERE IT WAS EMBRACED BY THE AZTEC PEOPLE, WHO HAD A SIMILAR CUSTOM.

popular with the Renaissance nobility. Instead of paper and seeds, small clay vessels were filled with trinkets and other pricier gifts, then batted at during pre-Lenten celebrations. Larger, colorful pignattas filled with candies were hung in town squares and smashed open for children during the carnival festivities.

The route from Italy to Spain brought small changes to the custom, which then made its way across the Atlantic with Spanish missionaries.

In Mexico, the Spanish piñatas were used as a tool of religious conversion, as the hanging pot was meant to represent sin, and those who destroyed it represented good vanquishing evil. Piñatas were readily accepted in Mexico because a similar Aztec ceremony honoring Huitzilopotchli, the god of war, already existed there.

by Heather Whipps

What Is Passover?

Passover is one of the most important holidays of the Jewish faith, an eight-day commemoration that overlaps in date with Easter.

It is commonly known that Passover marks the exodus of Hebrew slaves, led by Moses, from ancient Egypt. They eat only unleavened bread during the holiday because the Israelites left Egypt in such a hurry they could not wait for their bread to rise.

The name Passover, however, doesn't refer to passing over the matzo at the dinner table. According to the book of Exodus in the Old Testament, in which the Passover story is told, the God of the

IN THE 10TH PLAGUE THAT THE EGYPTIANS EXPERIENCED IN THE BOOK OF EXODUS IN THE BIBLE, MOSES INSTRUCTED THE ISRAELITES TO SMEAR LAMB'S BLOOD ON THEIR FRONT DOORS AS A SIGN TO THE ANGEL OF DEATH. THE SPIRIT WOULD KNOW TO "PASS OVER" THE HOUSEHOLDS WHO HAD DONE SO. HOWEVER, THE FIRST-BORN SONS OF THE EGYPTIANS WHO DID NOT OBEY THE WARNING, INCLUDING THE PHARAOH'S SON, PERISHED.

Israelites inflicted a series of 10 plagues on the Egyptians for their refusal to free the slaves. The tenth would be the slaying of the firstborn child of every Egyptian family. With insider information from the Big Man himself, Moses told the Israelites about the coming final plague and how to prepare for it. They were to cover their doors with a smear of lamb's blood as a signal to the angel of death to spare their homes.

Thus, all of the firstborn Jews of Egypt were passed over by death, and the intact families fled across the Red Sea.

Today, Passover is celebrated with a ritual meal called the Seder, featuring unleavened bread, during which the exodus story is often told.

by Heather Whipps

Why Is Friday the 13th Considered Unlucky?

o one knows for sure what's up with our odd fear of Friday the 13th, so ingrained in pop culture that it has a movie series and one mouthful of a phobia name—paraskavedekatriaphobia.

Folklorists think the dread goes back at least a few centuries, and may well trace its roots all the way to biblical times, when the 13th guest at the Last Supper betrayed Jesus and caused his Crucifixion, which was held on a Friday. Whatever the origin, by the late Middle Ages both Friday and the number 13 were considered bearers of misfortune. That potent combo, more than any specific association with the date, is what has deemed Friday the 13th unlucky.

THE FEAR OF FRIDAY THE 13TH IS CALLED PARASKAVEDEKATRIAPHOBIA.

Today it's dismissed as an old superstition but—if given a choice—how many of us would eschew getting married, flying or giving birth on a Friday the 13th? Superstition, indeed.

by Heather Whipps

Who Created Uncle Sam?

ames Montgomery Flagg created the iconic drawing of Uncle Sam. Flagg, an illustrator and portrait artist best known for his commercial art, contributed 46 works in support of the war effort during World War I. *Leslie's Weekly* first published his illustration of Uncle Sam as the cover of the July 6, 1916, issue with the title, "What Are You Doing for Preparedness?"

More than four million copies were printed between 1917 and 1918. The image also was used extensively during World War II.

In 1961, Congress passed a resolution that officially recognized meat packer Samuel Wilson (1766-1854) as Uncle Sam's namesake. Wilson, who supplied meat to the army during the War of 1812, is reputed to have been a man of great fairness, reliability, and honesty who was devoted to his country.

SAMUEL WILSON (1766-1854), A MEAT SUPPLIER TO THE ARMY DURING THE WAR OF 1812, WAS OFFICIALLY RECOGNIZED BY CONGRESS AS UNCLE SAM'S NAMESAKE IN 1961.

by Life's Little Mysteries *Staff*

What Do the Olympic Rings Symbolize?

The meaning of the Olympic Games' five interlocking rings is not at all black and white.

The rings of blue, black, yellow, red and green, which make up one of the most recognized symbols in the world, traditionally represent the five different areas of the world involved in the Olympics. North and South America are considered one area, along with Africa, Australia, Asia and Europe.

The International Olympic Committee states that the Olympic Symbol reinforces the international component of the Olympic Movement as the meeting of athletes from around the world. According to the Olympic Charter, "The Olympic symbol expresses the activity of the Olympic Movement and represents the union of the five continents and the meeting of athletes from throughout the world at the Olympic Games."

> THE FIVE RINGS SYMBOLIZE THE FIVE DIFFERENT AREAS OF THE WORLD INVOLVED IN THE OLYMPICS. NORTH & SOUTH AMERICA ARE CONSIDERED ONE AREA, ALONG WITH AFRICA, AUSTRALIA, ASIA AND EUROPE. ALTHOUGH THE RINGS ARE DIFFERENT COLORS, EACH AREA HAS NOT BEEN ASSIGNED A PARTICULAR COLOR.

But the six colors, if you include the white background in the Olympic flag, were intended to represent the various colors seen on the flags of nations competing in the Games of Olympiads I, II, III, IV and V. And historian David Young says it is likely that these rings could also symbolize the previous five Olympiads completed prior to 1914.

The 1928 St. Moritz winter games in Switzerland were the first to display the Olympic rings on the official Olympic poster. But it was not until the 1936 Summer Olympics in Berlin that this emblem became widely popular.

As an image of Olympism, Coubertin thought the rings had deep significance, that of the union of humanity.

American historian Robert Barney says, in his November 1992 article "The Great Symbol" published in *Olympic Review* (the official publication of the International Olympic Committee), that the roots of inspiration for the rings came from Coubertin's previous work.

In 1890, Coubertin became president of the Union des Sociétés Francaises des Sports Athlétiques (USFSA), a French sports-governing body. The USFSA arose as a result of a merger between two French sporting bodies, one led by Coubertin. To represent this merger, the USFSA had created a logo of two interlocking rings that was displayed on the uniforms of USFSA athletes starting in 1893—one year before Coubertin initiated the Sorbonne Conference in Paris where the Modern Olympic Movement began.

The larger symbolism of circles was likely not lost on Coubertin either. Circles, or rings, represent wholeness, according to psychologist Karl Jung, and when joined together, continuity.

by Greg Soltis

Chapter 4
Earth

      Earth, the third planet in our solar system and our home,
is mysterious. At 6 billion years old, the maternal body is an organism
itself, celebrated in Greek mythology as Gaia. Hurricanes and tornados
occur because of a chain of events that originate from the gravitational
pull of the sun and moon. Volcanoes and earthquakes result from internal
forces that move Earth's tectonic plates slowly over time. In this chapter,
we reveal answers to Earth's mysteries from the scientific community.

What's the Oldest Living Single Organism?

or most creatures, life is fleeting. An adult mayfly lives only 30 minutes. Humans make it an average of only 60 or 70 years; the current record holder is a woman who lived to 122 years. Galápagos tortoises top out at 190 years; some whales reach somewhere around 200. But for plants, life can stretch out many times that of animals. Trees often live for hundreds of years, with some truly ancient specimens standing sentry for millennia.

The oldest known living organism is a bristlecone pine that grows in southeastern California's White Mountains, says Ecologist Christopher Earle. A count of the tree's rings confirms that Methuselah, as the tree is affectionately known, is 4,841 years old. That's older than most of human civilization: Methuselah (the name of a man in the Bible who lived to be 969 years) sprouted during the Bronze Age, some two millennia before Rome was founded and a few hundred years before Egyptians constructed the Great Pyramid of Giza.

> THE LOCATION OF METHUSELAH, A 4,841 YEAR~OLD BRISTLECONE PINE, IS KEPT SECRET BY THE U.S. FOREST SERVICE TO PREVENT VANDALISM.

It's not uncommon for bristlecones to reach such an advanced age. According to the U.S. Forest Service, trees like Methuselah experience exceptionally slow growth in cold temperatures, which makes their wood dense and resistant to disease. Scientists have shown that bristlecones change little as they grow older and may not deteriorate with age the way other plants and organisms do.

Of course, getting to your 4,841st birthday takes a little luck. A bristlecone pine more than 100 years older than Methuselah was discovered in 1964 by researchers in Nevada. But its age—about 4,900 at the time—was only discovered after the tree, now called "Prometheus," was cut down. For this reason, the Forest Service keeps Methuselah's exact location secret from the public. It is likely that bristlecone pines more than 5,000 years old exist, but it may not be possible to measure their ages because old trees can lose their bark, allowing early rings to be worn away by wind and weather, Earle says.

Other species of trees grow even older than the bristlecone, but they need to cheat to get there: Certain species produce clones of themselves, with several generations of offshoots living out successive lifetimes from the same root system. A spruce tree in the Dalarna province of Sweden is the latest in a string of genetically identical clones stretching back 9,550 years. In southern Utah, a group of quaking aspen clones has been aged at 80,000 years, though none of the individual trees make it much past 75.

by Molika Ashford

Will an Asteroid Hit Earth? Are We All Doomed?

uestions about asteroids are frequent submissions to *Life's Little Mysteries*. Often they come from people who are really, really worried (and you can blame the media for the outsized concerns).

So first things first: Don't worry. Now for the answer: Yes. And no.

Yes, an asteroid will hit Earth. In fact, ten of them as big as refrigerators streak into the atmosphere every year. Most burn up on the way in, and about two-thirds of the rest (or chunks of them) fall harmlessly into the ocean (because the planet is about two-thirds ocean). Many smaller rocks plunge to the surface routinely (interestingly, about one rock from Mars arrives on Earth each month).

Some of these rocky extraterrestrials hit land but do little if any notable damage. The Meteor Crater in Arizona is a big exception, but that was 50,000 years ago. Now and then a piece from a space rock plunges through someone's roof.

There are no credible reports of anyone ever being killed, however. A horse in Ohio is said to have died in this way, but that was way back in 1860.

And yes, a larger deadly asteroid could eventually strike. However, a continent-destroying asteroid is not likely to hit during your lifetime. Most of the 1,100 or so that could do the job have been found.   A n d none are on their way. Okay, there is one mid-sized rock—called Apophis—that has a small chance of striking Earth in 2036 and wreaking some regional havoc. But astronomers are watching it and, if future observations reveal it really could hit us, scientists are confident they can devise a mission to deflect it. If all else fails, some futurists suggest that humanity could simply set up shop elsewhere.

> TEN ASTEROIDS AS BIG AS REFRIGERATORS ENTER EARTH'S ATMOSPHERE EACH YEAR, BUT ONLY A FRACTION OF THEM HIT THE EARTH'S SURFACE.

The real worry, if you want to worry about something, comes from comets.

Unlike asteroids, which orbit the Sun mostly in a neat belt between Mars and Jupiter and are relatively easy to find, comets hide in the far outskirts of the solar system. When they venture our way, we typically don't know about them until they are nearly upon us. Still, the odds are you're more likely to be killed by a dog, or by legal execution or by simply falling down than by being struck by any sort of space rock.

by Robert Roy Britt

Will California Ever Fall into the Ocean?

f plate tectonics followed the laws of Hollywood physics, Los Angeles would be tearing violently away from the mainland as we speak. The scenario would probably include a buxom seismologist and a secret nuclear warhead, too.

But rest assured that, outside of the movies, California Island won't be popping up on any maps. The San Andreas Fault, an 800-mile fracture in the Earth's crust stretches from the Gulf of California in the south to Mendocino in northern California, where it continues under the ocean. The fault is caused by two immense plates of rock, floating on a semi-molten layer, which meet and move against each other in what's called a strike-slip fault. The stress caused by this movement can result in devastating earthquakes, like the 1906 quake that destroyed much of San Francisco.

> THE MOTION BETWEEN THESE TWO ROCK MASSES BENEATH THE GOLDEN STATE IS MOSTLY HORIZONTAL. THAT IS, THE PACIFIC PLATE IS MOVING "UP" THE COAST, NOT "AWAY" FROM THE NORTH AMERICAN PLATE, AT A RATE OF DOZENS OF MILLIMETERS PER YEAR.

But the motion between these two rock masses beneath the Golden State is mostly horizontal. That is, the Pacific plate is moving "up" the coast, not "away" from the North American plate, at a rate of dozens of millimeters per year.

So in several million years, residents of Los Angeles will see the San Francisco skyline out their windows.

by Ben Mauk

Where Are the Oldest Rocks on Earth Found?

You don't need to go to a museum to find really, really old things. Ordinary rocks, for example, may be millions or billions of years old, and are free for the taking. But rocks you're likely to find along a nature trail or highway are mere infants compared to the oldest rocks on Earth.

Finding the oldest rocks in the world is a harder task than it might seem. Earth's crust is a dynamic system and is always in motion, so rocks are continually being moved around, created and melted down in the great geological recycling program. The oldest rocks on Earth can be very difficult to find and to verify, but the youngest rocks are easy to locate: look for the nearest active volcano.

TECHNICALLY, THE OLDEST KNOWN ROCKS EXISTING ON EARTH ARE NOT FROM EARTH AT ALL, BUT ARE INSTEAD OF EXTRATERRESTRIAL ORIGIN. MOON ROCK SAMPLES COLLECTED DURING THE APOLLO MISSIONS HAVE BEEN DATED TO ABOUT 4.5 BILLION YEARS, BESTING OUR OLDEST TERRESTRIAL ROCKS BY A FEW HUNDRED MILLION YEARS.

The oldest whole rocks found so far date back about 4.28 billion years. They were found in 2001 by geologists excavating near Canada's Hudson Bay in northern Quebec, according to the journal *Science*.

The oldest geological material ever found are mineral grains called zircons found in Western Australia, which date back about 4.36 billion years.

Technically, the oldest known rocks existing on Earth are not from Earth at all, but are instead of extraterrestrial origin. Moon rock samples collected during the Apollo missions have been dated to about 4.5 billion years, besting our oldest terrestrial rocks by a few hundred million years.

by Benjamin Radford

GEOLOGISTS CATEGORIZE ROCKS INTO THREE BASIC TYPES DEPENDING ON THEIR ORIGIN.

- IGNEOUS ROCKS ARE FORMED BY THE COOLING AND SOLIDIFICATION OF MAGMA (MOLTEN ROCK IN EARTH'S CRUST) ON OR NEAR THE SURFACE.

- SEDIMENTARY ROCKS, SUCH AS SANDSTONE, ARE CREATED BY THE COMPRESSION OF SEDIMENT OR PARTICLES.

- METAMORPHIC ROCKS ARE FORMED WHEN EXISTING IGNEOUS OR SEDIMENTARY ROCKS ARE FUSED TOGETHER BY HIGH HEAT AND PRESSURE.

Why Is the Sky Blue?

The light coming from the sun is made of many colors, each of which has a different wavelength. The atmosphere affects how each color of light passes through, as the light waves encounter molecules, small water droplets and bits of dust.

Blue light has a short wavelength, and the particles in the air scatter it around, making the sky appear blue. Red light has a longer wavelength, which acts more strongly and is not scattered as much.

THE LIGHT COMING FROM THE SUN IS MADE OF MANY COLORS, EACH OF WHICH HAS A DIFFERENT WAVELENGTH. BLUE LIGHT HAS A SHORT WAVELENGTH, AND THE PARTICLES IN THE AIR SCATTER IT AROUND, MAKING THE SKY APPEAR BLUE.

Sunsets are red because in the evening, the light has more atmosphere to pass through to get to your eye, and only the strong red light can make it.

by Robert Roy Britt

What's the Largest Waterfall in the World?

he tallest waterfall in the world is Venezuela's Angel Falls, which plunges 3,212 feet (979 m), according to the National Geographic Society. The falls descend over the edge of Auyán-Tepuí, which means Devil's Mountain, a flat-topped elevated area of land with sheer cliff sides located in Canaima National Park in the Bolivar State of Venezuela.

Angel Falls is named after American explorer and bush pilot Jimmy Angel, who crashed his plane on Auyán-Tepuí in 1937. The waterfall is fed by the Churún River, which spills over the edge of the mountain, barely touching the cliff face. The height of the fall is so great that the stream of water atomizes into a cloud of mist, then trickles back together at the bottom of the plunge and continues on through a cascading run of rapids.

> VENEZUELA'S ANGEL FALLS PLUNGES 3,212 FEET (979 M) OVER THE EDGE OF THE AUYÁN-TEPUÍ, LOCATED IN CANAIMA NATIONAL PARK IN THE BOLIVAR STATE OF VENEZUELA.

Angel Falls' total height, which is more than a half-mile (almost 1 km), includes both the free-falling plunge and a stretch of steep rapids at its base. But even discounting these rapids, the falls' long uninterrupted drop of 2,648 feet (807 m) is still a record breaker and is around 15 times the height of North America's Niagara Falls, according to the World Waterfall Database (WWD), a website maintained by waterfall enthusiasts.

> THE ANIMATED MOVIE *UP* FEATURES ANGEL FALLS AND THE AMERICAN EXPLORER AND BUSH PILOT JIMMY ANGEL.

When it comes to volume, picking the top waterfall is a little trickier because there is no universal standard for designating a waterfall, according to the World Waterfalls Database. Some waterfalls consist of a single, sheer drop, while others include a more gentle cascade over rapids. Still others involve a combination of the two (like Angel Falls).

The WWD lists Inga Falls, an area of rapids on the Congo River in Africa, as the waterfall with the largest volume. More than 11 million gallons of water flow through Inga Falls each second. However, without a vertical drop of any significant drama, Inga Falls may not count as a waterfall under other classifications.

Of waterfalls that do include a vertical drop, the waterfall with the greatest volume is the 45-foot Khone Falls located on the border between Laos and Cambodia. Spilling two and a half million gallons of the Mekong River every second, Khone Falls' flow is nearly double the volume of Niagara Falls.

by Molika Ashford

What Causes the Tides?

ides may seem simple on the surface, but the ins and outs of tides confounded great scientific thinkers for centuries—they even led Galileo astray into a bunk theory.

Current Moon Phase. Today people know that the gravitational pulls between the earth, moon and sun dictate the tides. The moon, however, influences tides the most.

The moon's gravitational pull on the earth is strong enough to tug the oceans into bulge. If no other forces were at play, shores would experience one high tide a day as the earth rotates on its axis and coasts run into the oceans' bulge facing the moon.

However, inertia—the tendency of a moving object to keep moving—affects the earth's oceans too. As the moon circles the earth, the earth moves in a very slight circle too, and this movement is enough to cause a centrifugal force on the oceans. (It's centrifugal force that holds water in a bucket when you swing the bucket in an overhead arc.)

This inertia, or centrifugal force, causes the oceans to bulge on the opposite side facing the moon. While the moon's gravitational pull is strong enough to attract oceans into a bulge on the side of the earth facing the moon, it is not strong enough to overcome the inertia on the opposite side of the earth. As a result, the world's oceans bulge twice—once when they are on the side of Earth closest to the moon, and once when they are on the side farthest from the moon, according to the Wood's Hole Oceanographic Institution in Wood's Hole, Mass.

Geography complicates the tides, but many places on Earth experience just two high and two low tides every 24 hours and 50 minutes. (The extra 50 minutes is caused by the distance the moon moves each day as it orbits Earth).

The Sun and the Tides. "Solar tides" are caused by the sun's gravitational pull and are weaker than lunar tides. The sun is 27 million times more massive than the moon, but it is also 390 times farther away. As a result, the sun has 46 percent of the tide-generating forces (TGFs) that the moon has, according to the National Oceanic and Atmospheric Administration (NOAA). Solar tides are therefore often considered just variations on lunar tides.

> THE WORLD'S OCEANS BULGE TWICE. ONCE WHEN THEY ARE ON THE SIDE OF EARTH CLOSEST TO THE MOON, AND ONCE WHEN THEY ARE ON THE SIDE FARTHEST FROM THE MOON. THE MOON'S GRAVITATIONAL PULL ON THE EARTH IS STRONG ENOUGH TO TUG THE OCEANS INTO BULGE, AND INERTIA THE TENDENCY OF A MOVING OBJECT TO KEEP MOVING CAUSES THE OCEANS TO BULGE ON THE OPPOSITE SIDE.

Local geography can vary tide strength as well. Just north of the coast of Maine in Canada, the Bay of Fundy has a unique "funnel shape" with just the right geography to create the largest tides in the world. Water in the bay can rise more than 49 feet (15 m) or about as high as a four-story house.

FORCE, the Fundy Ocean Research Center for Energy, estimates the Bay of Fundy pushes 110 billion tons (100 billion metric tons) of water with every tide.

Recently, local leaders have moved to take advantage of the tides. In July, Maine's Governor John Baldacci and Nova Scotia's Premier Darrell Dexter signed a Memorandum of Understanding to share research and ideas regarding the use of tidal and offshore wind as a renewable energy source, according to *Business Weekly*.

Understanding Tides: Then and Now. When Galileo Galilei attempted to explain tides in 1595, he left the moon out of this theory and focused instead on just part of the story—his correct idea that the earth orbited the sun.

It wasn't until 1687, that Sir Isaac Newton explained that ocean tides result from gravitational attraction of both the sun and the moon.

by Lauren Cox

How Big Was the Biggest Hailstone Ever?

n June 22, 2003, chunks of ice the size of softballs rained down on Aurora, Neb. One, a jagged behemoth with a 7-inch (17.8-cm) diameter, entered the record books as the largest U.S. hailstone ever.

Although large in size, it didn't unseat the champion by weight, which fell in Coffeyville, Kan., in 1970, according to the National Center for Atmospheric Research (NCAR). That hailstone weighed more than a pound and a half (0.75 kg).

So how do balls of ice bigger than a grapefruit form out of thin air? The answer is in the wind. Hail forms in the upper reaches of thunder clouds. Super-cooled water comes into contact with an ice crystal or dust particle and freezes, forming the core of a hailstone.

> SOME OF THE LARGEST HAILSTONES CAN FORM WHEN LOTS OF LITTLE HAILSTONES START TO MELT AND THEN FREEZE BACK TOGETHER IN THE ATMOSPHERE.

Upward-blowing winds called updrafts keep the tiny hailstone aloft. As it hovers in the cloud, the hailstone core acquires more layers of ice. The stronger the updrafts, the more layers the hailstone can accumulate before it falls to the earth and the larger it gets.

Some of the largest hailstones can also form when lots of little hailstones start to melt and then freeze back together in the atmosphere.

Updrafts blowing at 20 mph (32 kph) are capable of producing pea-sized hailstones, while winds twice as strong can create quarter-sized hail with a 1-inch (2.5 cm) diameter.

And as for the softball-sized hailstones that tore apart gutters and left craters in Nebraska cornfields in 2003? Those formed in a tempest with updrafts of at least 100 mph (160 kph).

by Stephanie Pappas

How Hot Is Lava?

Ice melts at 32°F (0°C). Chocolate melts at 90°F (32°C). But rock? Now we're talking a lot more heat.

Lava, the melted rock that shoots out of volcanoes, can flow at temperatures of thousands of degrees Fahrenheit.

Lava that's on the cooler side comes out of volcanoes at only pizza oven-like temperatures of 570°F (299°C), according to the United States Geological Survey (USGS).

In the middle range of lava temperatures, the dark red lava often seen slowly crawling across parts of Hawaii, measures around 895°F (479°C). Mount St. Helens ejected material of a similar temperature, although this material flew from the mountain at 100 mph, according to USGS.

THE TEMPERATURE OF LAVA CAN VARY. DARK RED LAVA MEASURES AROUND 895 F. BRIGHT RED LAVA CAN GET AS HOT AS 1,165 F.

However, once a volcano gets going, the mercury really starts to climb. Bright red lava that flows in Hawaii can get as hot as 1,165°F (629°C), with the glowing orange flows getting hotter than 1,600°F (871°C), according to USGS.

And when rock is seriously melting, such as the magma within the Hawaiian volcano of Kilauea, it can reach 2,120°F (1,160°C), according to USGS.

by Stuart Fox

What's the World's Biggest Glacier?

he world's largest glacier is the Lambert glacier in Antarctica, according to the U.S. Geological Survey. The glacier is more than 60 miles (96 km) wide at its widest point, about 270 miles (435 km) long, and has been measured to be 8,200 feet (2,500 m) deep at its center.

Glaciers form when the annual snowfall in a region exceeds the rate at which the snow melts, allowing enormous amounts of snow to accumulate over time. The fallen snow compresses into solid ice under its own weight, forming solid sheets of ice.

And these sheets are in motion. Glaciers flow like very slow-moving rivers, and can stretch over hundreds of miles. The Lambert glacier flows at a rate of about 1,300 to 2,600 feet (400 to 800 m) each year.

Although most of the world's glaciers are found in the Arctic and Antarctic regions, glaciers exist on all of the world's continents, according to the

> GLACIERS FORM WHEN THE ANNUAL SNOWFALL IN A REGION EXCEEDS THE RATE AT WHICH THE SNOW MELTS, ALLOWING ENORMOUS AMOUNTS OF SNOW TO ACCUMULATE OVER TIME. THE FALLEN SNOW COMPRESSES INTO SOLID ICE UNDER ITS OWN WEIGHT, FORMING SOLID SHEETS OF ICE.

National Snow and Ice Data Center at the University of Colorado at Boulder. Glaciers cover about 10 percent of the world's total land area.

by Karen Rowan

What Is the Great Barrier Reef?

 ustralia's Great Barrier Reef is the largest living organism on the planet, stretching some 1,430 miles (2,300 km). Home to 400 coral species, the Great Barrier Reef is a mosaic of approximately 2,900 offshore and inshore reefs. For comparison, the 135,000-square-mile reef ecosystem is about the size of Germany.

A coral reef consists of coral polyps, which are animals in the jellyfish family, along with algae called zooxanthellae. In return for a cozy, safe place to live, the algae provide the building blocks polyps need to survive and make limestone to build the reef structures. And the vast structures that result do more than awe snorkelers.

The reefs are vital to the survival of several endangered species, so much so that in 2004, the Great Barrier Reef Marine Park Authority increased the amount of highly protected zones by almost 30 percent.

A tourism hotspot, approximately 2 million people visit the Great Barrier Reef every year, according to the Australian government. There is widespread concern that such intense tourism might be harming the fragile reefs.

> **THE GREAT BARRIER REEF SUPPORTS A VAST ARRAY OF LIFE FORMS, INCLUDING:**
>
> - 5,000 MOLLUSK SPECIES (SUCH AS GIANT CLAMS)
> - 1,500 FISH SPECIES
> - 215 SPECIES OF BIRDS
> - 30 SPECIES OF WHALES, DOLPHINS AND PORPOISES
> - 14 SPECIES OF SEA SNAKES
> - 6 BREEDING SEA TURTLE SPECIES

Pollution is another concern, as an oil spill occurred on April 4, 2010 when the Chinese coal-carrying ship Shen Neng1 ran aground on the reef, leaking a 1.86-mile-long (3 km) ribbon of oil and destroying precious coral and marine life.

Declining water quality is also a major factor in the pollution of the Great Barrier Reef. During tropical floods, runoff containing fertilizer and pesticides is dispensed into the reef's waters and harms its delicately balanced ecosystem. The runoff problem is made worse by the loss of coastal wetlands along the Queensland coast, which act as a natural filter for toxins. The area of wetlands in the Great Barrier Reef catchment has decreased by over 50 percent since European settlement, according to the Great Barrier Reef Coastal Wetlands Protection Program.

by Remy Melina

> A CORAL REEF CONSISTS OF CORAL POLYPS, WHICH ARE ANIMALS IN THE JELLYFISH FAMILY, ALONG WITH ALGAE CALLED ZOOXANTHELLAE. IN RETURN FOR A COZY, SAFE PLACE TO LIVE, THE ALGAE PROVIDE THE BUILDING BLOCKS POLYPS NEED TO SURVIVE.

How Long Does it Take to Make Petrified Wood?

In Greek mythology, merely glancing at the ugly head of Medusa could turn the looker into stone. For wood, the process is not so fast.

Petrified wood forms when fallen trees get washed down a river and buried under layers of mud, ash from volcanoes and other materials. Sealed beneath this muck deprives the rotting wood from oxygen—the necessary ingredient for decay. As the wood's organic tissues slowly break down, the resulting voids in the tree are filled with minerals such as silica—the stuff of rocks.

Over millions of years, these minerals crystallize within the wood's cellular structure forming the stone-like material known as petrified wood. The wood, no longer wood at this point, takes on the hues of the minerals that fill its pores. Minerals such as copper, cobalt, and chromium give off a green-blue color, while manganese presents a pink hue.

by Michelle Bryner

Chapter 5
Space

The universe is a big, black, silent place full of cosmic explosions and space rocks thrust into the unknown by various forces. For centuries, astronomers and physicists have been trying to explain the phenomena found in outer space using high-level mathematical equations. In this chapter, we have compiled some less complicated answers.

What's the Difference Between an Asteroid and a Comet?

n asteroid is a body of rock smaller than 600 miles (1,000 km) in diameter—usually composed of carbon or metals—that orbits the sun. Most of our solar system's asteroids live in the asteroid belt between Mars and Jupiter. Although there are millions of asteroids in the belt, and several hundred with a diameter greater than 60 miles (100 km), the mass of all of them clumped together would be less than five percent of our moon.

Comets, such as Comet Harley 2, are balls of dirt and ice that are formed in the Kuiper Belt or the Oort Cloud. Comets orbit the sun but have much larger orbits than asteroids, whose orbits are generally more elliptical, or oval-shaped. As comets near the sun, solar energy begins to vaporize the ice, which creates their signature tails.

> MOST OF OUR SOLAR SYSTEM'S ASTEROIDS LIVE IN THE ASTEROID BELT BETWEEN MARS AND JUPITER. THERE ARE MILLIONS OF ASTEROIDS IN THE BELT, AND SEVERAL HUNDRED WITH A DIAMETER GREATER THAN 60 MILES (100 KM).

There are also substantial differences between meteoroids, meteors, and meteorites. A meteoroid, according to the International Astronomical Union, is a solid object moving in interplanetary space, of a size considerably smaller than an asteroid and considerably larger than an atom. In most cases, a meteor is debris from an asteroid collision. A meteor is simply a meteoroid that has entered Earth's atmosphere. (These typically burn up and create streaks through the sky, which earned meteors their "shooting star" nickname.) And a meteorite is a meteor that survives the atmosphere's burn and lands on the planet.

by Bjorn Carey

Are We Really All Made of Stars?

he theory that everyone and everything on Earth contains minuscule star particles dates back further than Moby's popular 2002 song, "We Are All Made of Stars."

In the early 1980s, Astronomer Carl Sagan hosted and narrated a 13-part television series called "Cosmos" that aired on PBS. On the show, Sagan thoroughly explained many science-related topics, including Earth's history, evolution, and the origin of life and the solar system.

"We are a way for the universe to know itself. Some part of our being knows this is where we came from. We long to return. And we can, because the cosmos is also within us. We're made of star stuff," Sagan famously stated in one episode.

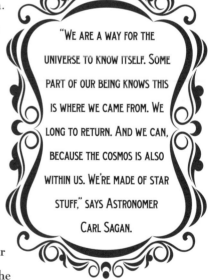

"WE ARE A WAY FOR THE UNIVERSE TO KNOW ITSELF. SOME PART OF OUR BEING KNOWS THIS IS WHERE WE CAME FROM. WE LONG TO RETURN. AND WE CAN, BECAUSE THE COSMOS IS ALSO WITHIN US. WE'RE MADE OF STAR STUFF," SAYS ASTRONOMER CARL SAGAN.

His statement sums up the fact that the carbon, nitrogen and oxygen atoms in our bodies, as well as atoms of all other heavy elements, were created in previous generations of stars over 4.5 billion years ago. Because humans and every other animal—as well as most of the matter on Earth—contain these elements, we are literally made of star stuff, says Chris Impey, professor of astronomy at the University of Arizona.

"All organic matter containing carbon was produced originally in stars," Impey tells *Life's Little Mysteries*. "The universe was originally hydrogen and helium. The carbon was made subsequently over billions of years."

How Star Stuff Got to Earth. When it has exhausted its supply of hydrogen, a star can die in a violent explosion called a nova. The explosion of a massive star, called a supernova, can be billions of times brighter than the Sun, according to *Supernova*, a book published by World Book Inc. Such a stellar explosion throws a large cloud of dust and gas into space. The amount and composition of the material expelled varies depending on the type of supernova.

A supernova reaches its peak brightness a few days after it first occurs, during which time it may outshine an entire galaxy of stars. The dead star then continues to shine intensely for several weeks before gradually fading from view.

The material from a supernova eventually disperses throughout interstellar space. The oldest stars almost exclusively consisted of hydrogen and helium, with oxygen and the rest of the heavy elements in the universe later coming from supernova explosions, according to *Cosmic Collisions; The Hubble Atlas of Merging Galaxies* published by Springer.

"THE UNIVERSE WAS ORIGINALLY HYDROGEN AND HELIUM. THE CARBON WAS MADE SUBSEQUENTLY OVER BILLIONS OF YEARS," SAYS CHRIS IMPEY, PROFESSOR OF ASTRONOMY AT THE UNIVERSITY OF ARIZONA.

"It's a well-tested theory," Impey says. "We know that stars make heavy elements, and late in their lives, they eject gas into the medium between stars so it can be part of subsequent stars and planets (and people)."

Cosmic Connections. So, all life on Earth and the atoms in our bodies were created in the furnace of now-long-dead stars, Impey says.

In 2002, music artist Moby released "We Are All Made of Stars." He explained during a press interview that his lyrics were inspired by quantum physics. "On a basic quantum level, all the matter in the universe is essentially made up of stardust," he said.

More recently, Symphony of Science, an artistic project headed by John Boswell designed to deliver scientific knowledge though musical remixes, released "We Are All Connected." The song, which features a clip of Sagan's "We're made of star stuff" proclamation, was created into a song with the software program Auto-Tune.

by Remy Melina

What's Hyperspace?

yperspace is the premise that it's possible to travel at speeds faster than that of light when energy from other dimensions is harnessed, and it is an idea used by many science fiction writers.

"If Captain Kirk were constrained to move at the speed of our fastest rockets, it would take him a hundred thousand years just to get to the next star system," says Seth Shostak, an astronomer at the Search for Extraterrestrial Intelligence (SETI) Institute in Mountain View, Calif. "Science fiction has long postulated a way to beat the speed of light barrier so the story can move a little more quickly."

But in reality, the concept is "a lot of hype," Shostak says.

The concept of hyperspace travel is also known as hyperdrive, subspace and warp speed.

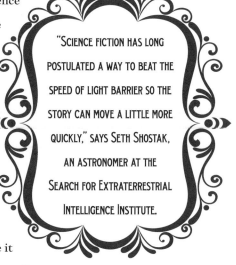

"SCIENCE FICTION HAS LONG POSTULATED A WAY TO BEAT THE SPEED OF LIGHT BARRIER SO THE STORY CAN MOVE A LITTLE MORE QUICKLY," SAYS SETH SHOSTAK, AN ASTRONOMER AT THE SEARCH FOR EXTRATERRESTRIAL INTELLIGENCE INSTITUTE.

But the dearth of research and scholarly discussion on the transportation method make it more often a convenient literary device than scientific possibility.

Other Dimensions. However, physics suggests that shortcuts through space do exist, Shostak says. The curved nature of space was first proposed by Einstein, and it quickly led to the idea of a wormhole: a portion of space that curves in on itself, connecting two otherwise distant parts of space. A spacecraft could theoretically skip ahead to a distant region of space if it enters such a wormhole between the two locations.

As in our familiar universe, objects in a wormhole would have to travel slower than the speed of light. But, a spaceship could appear to have exceeded this limit, by traveling through a wormhole and reaching a star system thousand of lights years away in a matter of hours, for example. However, our access to these inter-space freeways would be limited by the size of the portal.

"Wormholes, we think, are made all the time on a microscopic level," Shostak says. "But the question is, can we actually use them for transportation?"

Finding or creating a wormhole that's going to the right place and scooting through it before it closes up and smashes one to pieces are two unsolved problems that the laws of physics don't clearly bar or allow.

> TECHNICALLY, IT WOULD BE POSSIBLE TO WARP SPACE TO CREATE A WORMHOLE IF YOU COULD PLACE A VERY DENSE MASS IN FRONT OF YOUR ROCKETSHIP. THE OBJECT WOULD DISTORT THE SHAPE OF SPACE AROUND IT, BRINGING THE CHOSEN DESTINATION CLOSER TO THE SHIP. BUT THE OBJECT WOULD NEED TO HAVE THE DENSITY OF THE CENTER OF A BLACK HOLE IN ORDER TO WORK.

Technically, it would be possible to warp space to create a wormhole if you could place a very dense piece of mass in front of your rocketship. Perhaps similar to the "hyperspace engine" seen in the Star Wars movies, the object would distort the shape of space around it, essentially bringing the chosen destination closer to the ship. But the object would need to have the density of the center of a black hole in order to work.

"The problem is, where do you get the black hole and how do you get it in front of your spacecraft?" Shostak says. "It's sort of like, how do you create something that will warp space and then put it in front of your spacecraft?"

What About Teleportation? A related science fiction idea is teleportation—the possibility of instantly conveying a person or ship into another part of the universe.

The phenomenon is seen in *Star Trek*, where a so-called teleporter deconstructs one's body and reconstructs it at another, distant location.

There is some scientific basis for this idea—scientists have shown that subatomic particles can be moved from one point to another faster than the speed of light.
But the ability to break apart and reassemble an entire human appears impossible. Because of the randomized aspects behind the arrangement of subatomic particles, perfectly reversing them becomes increasingly difficult as they accumulate in greater numbers, says physicist Ian Durham at Saint Anselm College.

Star-Jumping, Within Limits. Still, the notion of hyperspace exists in science fiction for a reason: there's a big difference between traveling at nearly the speed of light and traveling over it.

Spaceships traveling at 99 percent the speed of light could reach a star several light years away within a person's lifetime, Shostak says.

But for cosmic bodies billions of light years away, such travel would still not be an option—the lifetimes of many generations of humans would be needed.

"As far as we know, traveling between the stars is either very hard or involves exploiting wormholes in a way we don't understand yet," Shostak says. "On the other hand, we have to remember that the universe continually surprises us with its subtlety."

by Zoe Macintosh

What's at the Center of the Milky Way?

f you look up on a dark, clear night, away from city lights, you may see a wide band of faint light stretching above you, stiller than a cloud and glittering with densely packed stars. Translated from the Ancient Greek as "Milky Way" for resembling spilled milk on the sky, that band of light is the center of our galaxy.

At its center, surrounded by 200-400 billion stars and undetectable to the human eye and by direct measurements, lies a supermassive black hole called Sagittarius A*, or Sgr A* for short.

The Milky Way has the shape of a spiral and rotates around its center, with long curling arms surrounding a slightly bulging disk. It's on one of these arms—close to the center—that the sun and Earth are located. Scientists estimate that the galactic center and Sgr A* are around 25,000 to 28,000 light years away from us.

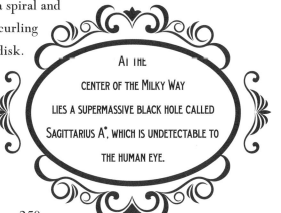

At the center of the Milky Way lies a supermassive black hole called Sagittarius A*, which is undetectable to the human eye.

We revolve around the center every 250 million years. While the supermassive black hole—the largest type of black hole in a galaxy, with a mass millions of times that of our Sun—can't be imaged directly because black holes pull in all light, scientists have inferred its presence by looking at the speed and motion of stars and matter close to the galactic center. They have inferred that the movements are influenced by the gravitational pull of a black hole.

No one knows how the black holes at the center of galaxies form, but some suspect they may begin as a cluster of smaller black holes that merge, or when a smaller black hole consumes enough matter to become a supermassive one.

by Kristina Grifantini

What Are Supernovas and What Do Scientists Learn From Them?

urning a billion times brighter than our sun, the phenomena called supernovas have unlocked mysteries about black holes, the origin of metals such as gold and the expansion of the universe.

Supernovas are rare—the last supernova seen in our galaxy was recorded in 1604, according to NASA.

This supernova may have baffled those living at the time, but by observing supernovas in other galaxies, astronomers now understand what a supernova is—the final explosion of a massive, dying star.

What Happens During a Supernova. All stars, including our sun, will eventually run out of the hydrogen gas that fuels the nuclear fusion reactions in their cores. When this happens, smaller stars expand into what astronomers call red giants, then shrink into faint white dwarfs.

But "massive" stars, that have at least five times the mass of the sun, are likely to become red supergiants that explode as supernovas.

Forces at work within stars are what give rise to the explosion seen during supernovas. For most of a star's life, gravity pulls its gases inward, but its nuclear reactions push the gases outward, and the forces engage in a constant tug-of-war. But when the nuclear fusion in a star stops, the star loses the outward push that counters gravity. Gravity then takes over, and the star begins to collapse in on itself.

Eventually, the force of the collapsing material heats up the star's core enough to start a series of new nuclear reactions, forming heavier and heavier metals, until the core becomes solid iron and nuclear reactions stop.

Within a second, the iron core's temperature rises to more than 180 billion degrees Fahrenheit (100 billion degrees Celsius), crushing the iron atoms closer together until the core explodes in a shock wave. This explosion is a supernova.

Supernovas may leave behind a brilliantly colored cloud of gas called a nebula, a black hole or perhaps nothing at all.

But that just explains Type II supernovas. Type I supernovas involve a complex interaction between a pair of a "binary stars" where one star eventually explodes, according to NASA.

What Supernovas Reveal. In February 2006, researchers observed an unusual supernova 440 million light years away. As it exploded, the supernova released an intense flash of X-rays called a gamma-ray burst. Previously, scientists thought gamma ray bursts only formed from spiraling matter falling into black holes. As more research is done into supernovas, scientists have also used the phenomena to study the entire universe.

> THE LAST SUPERNOVA SEEN IN OUR GALAXY WAS RECORDED IN 1604. THIS SUPERNOVA MAY HAVE BAFFLED THOSE LIVING AT THE TIME, BUT BY OBSERVING SUPERNOVAS IN OTHER GALAXIES, ASTRONOMERS NOW UNDERSTAND WHAT A SUPERNOVA ISBTHE FINAL EXPLOSION OF A MASSIVE, DYING STAR.

A subtype of supernovas, Type Ia, are among the brightest things in the universe, and all shine with roughly equal intensity. So by observing supernovas over time, researchers in the 1990s were able to see that the supernovas were all moving away from the center of the universe at an increasing rate, showing that the universe is expanding. Scientists call the unknown force behind the expansion dark energy.

In April 2010, the international Supernova Cosmology Project (SCP) at the Lawrence Berkeley National Laboratory announced the largest collection of data on supernovas yet amassed, to continue studying dark energy.

by Lauren Cox

Why Are Space Telescopes Better than Earth-Based Telescopes?

 he Hubble Telescope has beamed hundreds of thousands of images back to Earth over the past two decades. One might call it the most skilled paparazzo, snapping countless images of the stars.

Thanks to these images, scientists have been able to determine the age of the universe and shed light on the existence of dark energy. These extraordinary advancements have been possible because the Hubble images surpass those taken by Earth-based telescopes.

While ground-based observatories are usually located in highly elevated areas with minimal light pollution, they must contend with atmospheric turbulence, which limits the sharpness of images taken from this vantage point. (The effects of atmospheric turbulence are clear to anyone looking at the stars—this is why they appear to twinkle.)

In space, however, telescopes are able to get a clearer shot of everything from exploding stars to other galaxies.

Another disadvantage for ground-based telescopes is that the Earth's atmosphere absorbs much of the infrared and ultraviolet light that pass through it. Space telescopes can detect these waves.

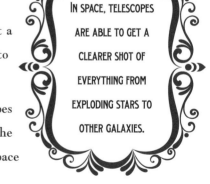

IN SPACE, TELESCOPES ARE ABLE TO GET A CLEARER SHOT OF EVERYTHING FROM EXPLODING STARS TO OTHER GALAXIES.

Newer ground-based telescopes using technological advances such as adaptive optics to try to correct or limit atmospheric distortion, but there's no way to see the wavelengths that the atmosphere blocks from reaching Earth, according to the Space Telescope Science Institute (STScI).

One downside to space telescopes like the Hubble is that they are extremely difficult to maintain and upgrade. The Hubble is the first telescope specifically designed to be repaired in space by astronauts. Other space telescopes cannot be serviced at all.

NASA scientists estimate that the telescope will only be able to keep taking pictures until 2015.

by Remy Melina

What Are Cosmic Rays?

The next time any of your electronics act up for no apparent reason, you might find that cosmic rays are to blame.

Cosmic rays are high-energy protons that originate in shock waves from the remnants of supernovas—the death heaves of giant exploded stars. Shells of gas are ejected from a star before it collapses in a supernova explosion, and these highly-magnetic remnants speed up the particles to form cosmic rays.

> COSMIC RAYS CONSTANTLY RAIN DOWN ON EARTH, AND WHILE THE HIGH-ENERGY "PRIMARY" RAYS COLLIDE WITH ATOMS IN THE EARTH'S UPPER ATMOSPHERE AND RARELY MAKE IT THROUGH TO THE GROUND, "SECONDARY" PARTICLES ARE EJECTED FROM THIS COLLISION AND DO REACH US ON THE GROUND.

Cosmic rays constantly rain down on Earth, and while the high-energy "primary" rays collide with atoms in the Earth's upper atmosphere and rarely make it through to the ground, "secondary" particles are ejected from this collision and do reach us on the ground.

Radiation emitted from these cosmic rays has been known to cause abnormal and often mysterious behavior in some electronics, depending on how sensitive or vulnerable the microprocessors or memory chips are to the particles' energy. Such abnormalities can be anything from data loss or altered programming, to much more serious corruptions of circuitry functions. Permanent damage is a possibility, though not always the case.

Radiation from cosmic rays is being closely studied in order to determine its harmful effects on various systems, including aircraft, satellites, biomedical systems and, most recently, automobiles.

by Denise Chow

Why Does Outer Space Look Black?

The color black usually signals the absence of light. But inside the solar system, space is filled with light.

"Light usually travels straight ahead in a line unless it reflects off something or is bent by a lens," explains Geza Gyuk, Director of Astronomy at the Adler Planetarium and a research scientist at the University of Chicago.

Think about how you can see the spot of a laser pointer but not the beam. "The light that makes up the beam just goes ahead to where the pointer is pointing and not to where your eye is," Gyuk says. "So even though space may be full of light, none makes its way to your eye unless you are looking at something bright."

So, Gyuk said, "Because most of the universe is empty, outer space looks black."

by Corey Binns

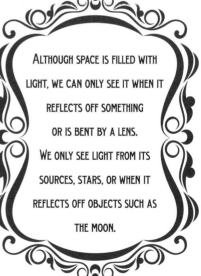

ALTHOUGH SPACE IS FILLED WITH LIGHT, WE CAN ONLY SEE IT WHEN IT REFLECTS OFF SOMETHING OR IS BENT BY A LENS. WE ONLY SEE LIGHT FROM ITS SOURCES, STARS, OR WHEN IT REFLECTS OFF OBJECTS SUCH AS THE MOON.

What Is the Largest Known Star?

The heftiest, brightest known star is in the Pistol Nebula and is located 25,000 light-years away in the direction of the constellation Sagittarius. It is believed to be 100 times as massive as our Sun, and 10 million times as bright. The Sun's mass is about 2×10^{27} tons, which is a 2 followed by 27 zeros, or 333,000 times as massive as Earth.

THE LARGEST GASEOUS SHELL IN THE PISTOL NEBULA IS SO BIG (4 LIGHT YEARS ACROSS) THAT IT WOULD STRETCH NEARLY ALL THE WAY FROM OUR SUN TO THE NEXT NEAREST STAR.

The brilliant star may have begun life weighing as much as 200 solar masses. Over time, however, it has violently shed much of its mass.

In fact, the radiant star has enough raw power to blow off two expanding shells of gas equal to the several solar masses. The largest shell is so big (4 light years) that it would stretch nearly all the way from our Sun to the next nearest star.

Despite its great distance from us, the Pistol Nebula would be a stellar sight if not for the dust between it and the Earth. Astronomers used the infrared camera on NASA's Hubble Space Telescope to peel away the obscuring dust and reveal the star.

Astronomers are currently unsure how a star this massive could have formed and how it will act in the future.

by Life's Little Mysteries *Staff*

How Was Our Solar System Formed?

cientists aren't completely sure how the solar system formed, but most agree the best explanation is that a cloud of molecules collapsed inward on itself, forming our solar system about 4.6 billion years ago.

In this description, called the nebular model, our Sun came together first, surrounded by a spinning disk of gas and dust.

How the Sun Formed. Some evidence, such as a 2010 study from scientists at the Carnegie institution, suggests this contraction could have been spurred by a burst from nearby supernovas. Other forces like differences in density could also have caused the cloud to begin collapsing, according to *From Suns to Life: A Chronological Approach to the History of Life on Earth* published by Springer.

> INITIALLY, GAS COLLECTED IN THE DENSE CENTER OF A SPINNING DISK OF MOLECULES, CREATING A PROTOSUN. COLLISIONS BETWEEN MOLECULES HEATED THINGS UP, EVENTUALLY RAISING TEMPERATURES TO ABOUT 10 MILLION DEGREES CELSIUS. THESE INCREASINGLY HOT AND VIOLENT CRASHES SPARKED NUCLEAR REACTIONS, WHICH TURNED THE PROTOSUN INTO A STAR.

Initially, gas collected in the dense center of this spinning disk, creating a protosun. Collisions between molecules heated things up, eventually raising temperatures to about 10 million degrees Celsius. These increasingly hot and violent crashes sparked nuclear reactions, which turned the protosun into a star. This process took about 100,000 years, according to *From Suns to Life*.

How the Planets Formed. Meanwhile, in the disk of material around the young sun, a process called accretion formed the planets, moons, comets and asteroids. Small particles crashed together to form larger and larger bodies, eventually reaching the size of planetesimals—up to a few kilometers across. Massive enough to create their own gravity, these bodies drew even more collisions, with only the largest surviving the destructive crashes, according to the Lunar and Planetary Institute.

In the hot area near the evolving Sun, water on the planetesimals tended to evaporate away, gases were swept outward and only heavier material, like silicon and metals could condense into solids. Young planets in the inner solar system (like Earth) formed from this rocky, dense material.

Farther away from the new star, cooler temperatures and abundant ice allowed for much larger bodies to form, creating the cores of planets such as Jupiter and Saturn. These cores were large enough for their gravity to pull in gas from the surrounding nebula, creating the gas giants of the outer solar system, according to the third edition of *The Solar System*, an astronomical reference book.

The Other Objects in the Solar System. Beyond Neptune, in the even colder reaches of the disk, there was not enough material available for planetesimals to grow to gas giants. These stunted chunks make up the Kuiper belt.

Between Mars and Jupiter, another field of planetesimals became the asteroid belt, which is thought to have been kept from clumping into a planet by the gravity of Jupiter, according to *The Solar System*.

The nebular model explains why all of the planets orbit in the plane of the Sun's rotation—that plane contains the remnants of that early gaseous disk.

Telescopes have captured images of early moments in the formation of other solar systems throughout the universe, showing in live action what we believe took place around our own Sun.

by Molika Ashford

What Is a Quasar?

he word "quasar" refers to a "quasi-stellar radio source." The first quasars were discovered in the 1960s when astronomers measured their very strong radio emissions. Later, scientists discovered that quasars are actually radio-quiet, with very little radio emission. However, quasars are some of the brightest and most distant objects we can see.

These ultra-bright objects are likely the centers of active galaxies where supermassive black holes reside. As material spirals into the black holes, a large part of the mass is converted to energy. It is this energy that we see. And though smaller than our solar system, a single quasar can outshine an entire galaxy of a hundred billion stars.

To date, astronomers have identified more than a thousand quasars.

QUASARS ARE ULTRA-BRIGHT OBJECTS THAT ARE LIKELY THE CENTERS OF ACTIVE GALAXIES WHERE SUPERMASSIVE BLACK HOLES RESIDE.

by Life's Little Mysteries *Staff*

What Does E=MC² Mean?

=MC² is a version of Einstein's famous Relativity equation. Specifically, it means that energy is equal to mass multiplied by the speed of light squared. While seemingly simple, this relativity equation has many profound implications, such as the rule that no object with mass can ever go faster than the speed of light.

That's because the total energy of an object increases as its speed increases. As an object's speed reaches the speed of light its mass approaches infinity. This means that it would take an infinite amount of energy to accelerate an object to the speed of light.

by Life's Little Mysteries *Staff*

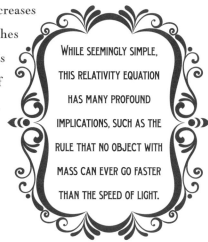

WHILE SEEMINGLY SIMPLE, THIS RELATIVITY EQUATION HAS MANY PROFOUND IMPLICATIONS, SUCH AS THE RULE THAT NO OBJECT WITH MASS CAN EVER GO FASTER THAN THE SPEED OF LIGHT.

Why Do Stars Twinkle?

Stars twinkle because their light must pass through pockets of Earth's atmosphere that vary in temperature and density, and it's all very turbulent. On rough nights, a star appears to shift position constantly as its light is refracted this way and that.

It's much like watching a coin appear to dance at the bottom of a pool. Astronomers try to overcome the twinkling by using adaptive optics, in which many small mirrors on the scope adjust constantly to allow for atmospheric disturbances.

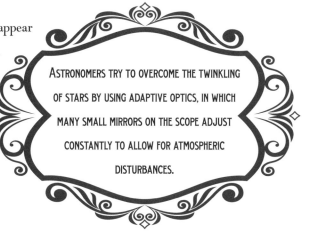

ASTRONOMERS TRY TO OVERCOME THE TWINKLING OF STARS BY USING ADAPTIVE OPTICS, IN WHICH MANY SMALL MIRRORS ON THE SCOPE ADJUST CONSTANTLY TO ALLOW FOR ATMOSPHERIC DISTURBANCES.

They can also use space-based telescopes to make observations. Telescopes orbiting Earth above the atmosphere avoid the problems caused by turbulence.

Planets, on the other hand, generally do not appear to twinkle. The planets of our solar system are much closer to Earth than the stars we see, so planets loom slightly larger within our field of vision (in reality, stars are actually much larger). Because planets appear larger, the light reflecting from them is less shifted around by the pockets of air in the turbulent upper atmosphere, according to astronomer and blogger Phil Plait.

But the rule is not hard and fast—planets can appear to twinkle when the atmosphere is unusually turbulent.

by Life's Little Mysteries *Staff*

Chapter 6
Entertainment

Movies, television shows, concerts, books and celebrity tracking play a huge role in our lives. Watching the longest-running TV magazine show *Entertainment Tonight* or reading about celebs in the grocery-store check-out line is a common pastime and the source of casual conversations for many. Celebrities almost become surrogate family members that keep us company and keep life interesting. This chapter includes entertainment facts that will likely bring back memories.

Which Band Headlined the First Stadium Rock Concert?

Stadium concerts are commonplace now in the music business.

Bruce Springsteen and the E Street Band, U2, Bon Jovi, Green Day and Kenny Chesney are just some of the artists who regularly play outdoor gigs at 70,000-seat football stadiums. But 45 years ago, the music business was turned on its ear by four mop-topped kids from Liverpool who put on a concert for the ages.

On Aug. 15, 1965, the Beatles became the first rock band to perform at an American sports stadium with their show at Shea Stadium in Queens, New York. Before a crowd of 55,000 crazed and mostly female fans, the Fab Four made history by playing some of their most popular songs on the home turf of the Mets and Jets.

Too bad most of the audience couldn't hear any of it. Hysteria ran so high that fans literally screamed throughout the band's 30-minute set.

The milestone in music history was captured in the documentary *The Beatles at Shea Stadium*, which was produced by Ed Sullivan's production company to document Beatlemania, which was then at its apex. A staple of the bootleg circuit for decades, the documentary showed the over-the-top fans on display that day at Shea. Security guards are seen covering their ears, and the band can't even hear itself play over the piercing shrieks.

> FANS IN ATTENDANCE "COULDN'T POSSIBLY HAVE HEARD ANYTHING BUT THEIR OWN SCREAMS" DURING THE CONCERT. "FOR THAT MATTER, THEY DIDN'T SEEM TO WANT TO," REPORTED THE *NEW YORK DAILY NEWS.*

The day after the concert, the *New York Daily News* featured what was perhaps one of its most matter-of-fact headlines ever, "55,000 Scream for Beatles."

The story said the fans in attendance "couldn't possibly have heard anything but their own screams" during the concert. "For that matter, they didn't seem to want to."

Part of the problem had to do with the layout of the concert. Unlike modern stadium shows, fans at the Beatles' Shea concert weren't allowed on the field. The band was on a stage in the outfield, far from the crowd. The stadium's primitive public-address sound system was no match for the decibel power of all those fans.

The noise issue continued to haunt the Beatles through the rest of the tour, which featured a handful of other stadium dates, and even on their 1966 return engagement to Shea Stadium. That 1966 tour would mark the end of the Beatles' touring days. Afterward, the band stayed in the studio until their breakup in 1970.

The 1965 concert at Shea may have been musically mediocre, but financially it was a game changer. The gate take-in was $304,000, the largest in music history to that point. By giving birth to stadium rock, the Beatles had done what they have done throughout their careers: change the music business.

Outdoor stadium shows are still windfalls for their promoters and bands. And with modern sound and lighting systems, bands such as U2 and the Rolling Stones have created unforgettable concert experiences for the fans in attendance.

It can all be traced back to that night in Queens in 1965, when the crowd drowned out the Beatles.

by Michael Avila

What Are the Best MacGyver Stunts?

he 2010 movie *MacGruber*, which brought the *Saturday Night Live* sketch featuring Will Forte and Kristen Wiig to movie screens this month, is a parody of the TV series *MacGyver* that ran during the 1980s and 1990s.

The show has such an avid cult following that the word "macgyverize" is included in the Merriam-Webster's open dictionary and is defined as, "to apply scientific or engineering knowledge in the inventive use of common items." *MacGyver*, which ran for seven seasons, inspired the phrase, "What would MacGyver do?" And fans can even buy an exact replica of MacGyver's trusty Swiss Army pocket knife. The utility knife has 16 functions, including a "laser" light and wood and rope saw.

> WITH THE THIN LAYER OF DUST EVENLY DISTRIBUTED OVER THE FINGERPRINT SENSOR'S PLATE, MACGYVER PLACES HIS JACKET OVER IT AND GENTLY PRESSES DOWN WITH HIS FINGERS TO FOOL THE SCANNER INTO RE~READING THE HAND PRINT OF THE LAST PERSON WHO USED IT, GRANTING MACGYVER ACCESS.

In honor of MacGyver, the secret agent and gun control advocate who can hotwire a car with a paper clip, create a radar-jamming device out of kitchen appliances and unblock nuclear reactor cooling systems using only a dismantled revolver as a wrench, we've put together the hero's top five coolest and most random stunts.

1. MacGyver Saves the Day with Chocolate. In the series' pilot, after MacGyver uses a paper clip to short-circuit a highly advanced timing device on a nuclear warhead and diffuse the bomb at the very last second, our hero comes back to save the day with chocolate. While using the sweet treat to plug up a sulfuric acid leak, he explains that, when mixed with acid, the sugars in chocolate form elemental carbon in a thick, gummy residue. In a segment called "Can Chocolate Stop Acid?" the *Mythbusters* crew used Hershey's chocolate bars to successfully recreate MacGyver's feat.

2. He Rescues Baby Eagles. MacGyver bravely hang-glides over the hills of Utah to protect a family of adorable eaglets from evil hunters who have killed the mother eagle in the "Eagles" episode. He then brings the rescued chicks to the safety of his house, where he builds them an incubator using just vegetable oil and the padding from a chair. Soaking the padding's fibers with the oil creates a chemical reaction that generates heat, according to MacGyver, which keeps the baby chicks cozy.

3. MacGyver Defeats Laser-Wielding Robots. Lasers are no match for MacGyver. He uses a clear strand from a fiber optic lamp to bend a security laser sensor just enough so that he can deftly slide by without triggering the alarm in an episode entitled, "The Heist." In "The Human Factor," MacGyver destroys two laser emitters at once by pushing a mirror attached to a cleaning cart at just the right angle to cause the lasers to reflect at each other. And in the same episode, he tricks laser-wielding robots into blowing each other up by attaching telephone handset magnets wrapped in burning paper to their metal torsos. The heat from the fire mimics body heat and makes the robots turn on each other in a flaming laser duel.

4. He Outsmarts a Handprint Scanner. In a move that was later copied by the Scooby-Doo gang, MacGyver uses dust to fake a handprint for an electronic scanning device. He first scrapes a plaster wall to produce the dust, and then completely covers the scanner in the powder, carefully blowing off any excess. With the thin layer of dust evenly distributed over the sensor's plate, MacGyver places his jacket over it and gently presses down with his fingers to fool the scanner into re-reading the hand print of the last person who used it, granting MacGyver access.

5. MacGyver plugs an oil leak. BP probably wishes they could have had MacGyver on their brainstorming team during the massive oil spill in the Gulf of Mexico, as he is able to fix a broken fuel line using only a ballpoint pen. When a small fuel line is punctured in an episode called "Three for the Road," MacGyver completely removes the damaged section by cutting it out. Using a hollowed-out pen, he reconnects the fuel line by sliding each loose end over the pen, forming a perfect, airtight seal.

by Remy Melina

When Did the Red Carpet Tradition Begin?

 alking the red carpet used to be a really big deal. But lately, it's become so watered-down that any jabroni on a reality show or seventh-billed actor on a mediocre sitcom gets to walk the carpet for fans and paparazzi.

Yes, the red carpet has certainly lost some of its mojo from its more stately origins as a way to honor gods and dignitaries. But before it became co-opted by Hollywood as self-aggrandizing promotion, the red carpet was actually something special.

The first known mention of a red carpet being rolled out goes all the way back to the 5th Century BC in Aeschylus' play *Agamemnon*. In the play, the Greek king's wife, Clytemnestra, prepared the carpet as a way to set up her philandering husband to be murdered by her own hands. Agamemnon walks the carpet laid out for his triumphant welcome—and promptly gets wacked. The following text comes from the play:

> THE SPECIAL RED-CARPET TREATMENT WAS FIRST MENTIONED IN AESCHYLUS' 5TH-CENTURY PLAY *AGAMEMNON*, WHERE HIS WIFE TRICKS HIM INTO WALKING ON THE CARPET RESERVED FOR THE GODS SO THAT SHE CAN MURDER HIM. THE CARPET WAS ORIGINALLY PURPLE BUT OVER TIME, THE RED CARPET TRADITION DEVELOPED.

"I am a mortal, a man; I cannot trample upon these tinted splendors without fear thrown in my path."

Agamemnon, aware of the tradition of laying out the carpet to honor the gods, was wary of disrespecting Zeus and his fellow deities. The King of Argos should have followed his first instinct.

Incidentally, the Greeks (and the Romans) were several thousand years ahead of the artist Prince when it came to loving purple. For the upper-echelon of Ancient Greece, purple was a measure of their Royalness. Scholars believe the carpet mentioned in *Agamemnon* was actually purple, but that the color has become confused over the centuries.

In modern times, President James Monroe in 1821 was honored at Prospect Hill (which is now known as Arcadia) on Waccamaw in South Carolina with a red carpet laid out to the river.

But what really cemented the red carpet tradition were the railroads. Passengers in New York and Chicago who rode the 20th Century Limited train walked on and off the train via a plush carpet, adding to the luxury and uniqueness of the trips.

Luxury and uniqueness is no longer the case. Every D-Lister and their DVD release gets the red carpet these days. Too bad Agamemnon's fears didn't survive the passage of time, like his story has.

by Michael Avila

Which Superheroes Don't Have Superpowers?

Many traditional superheroes in comics don't have superpowers. But that does not demean their superhero status.

Merriam-Webster defines "superhero" as "a fictional hero having extraordinary or superhuman powers." Intuitively, though, that seems incorrect. One of the most famous superheroes of all, Batman, has no powers to speak of, but still wears a mask and a cape, has a secret identity and prowls around his town at night looking for bad guys to beat up. Pretty much the superhero job description, right?

The dictionary continues, "also: an exceptionally skillful or successful person." Bruce Wayne is certainly both, though the relative ambiguity of the supplementary definition implies that any exceptionally skillful and successful person could be considered a superhero, cape or not. (Oprah Winfrey, superheroine?)

It's also important to look at the situations Batman, the most prominent, powerless, costumed crime-fighter, finds himself in—he's frequently fighting aliens and otherworldly beings, he built the Justice League, an outer space hangout, and there's an entire comic book series dedicated to his team-ups with Superman. It's amazing he has time to chase Two-Face out of abandoned Gotham City warehouses.

Clearly, Batman is more than compensating for his lack of powers with his superhero-like behavior. But not every powerless costumed crimefighter is a superhero. Take Marvel Comics' the Punisher, who also uses only his intellect (and a copious amount of guns and ammo) to fight crime, but usually does so solely against street-level thugs and mobsters.

> BATMAN, IRONMAN AND GREEN LANTERN DON'T HAVE SUPERPOWERS, AND YET THEY ARE STILL SUPERHEROES BECAUSE OF THEIR EXCEPTIONAL SKILLS AND SUCCESS. AND BATMAN, FOR EXAMPLE, IS ALWAYS GETTING HIMSELF INTO CHALLENGING SITUATIONS SUCH AS FIGHTING ALIENS AND OTHERWORLDLY BEINGS. HE ALSO TEAMS UP WITH SUPERMAN ON A REGULAR BASIS.

There's a whole class of DC Comics and Marvel characters that are superheroes merely by virtue of being really good at something, commonly archery. Green Arrow, his Marvel counterpoint Hawkeye, and Green Arrow's many associates and protégés (Arsenal, Speedy and Arrowette) all manage to be superheroes simply by being handy with a bow.

Marvel's Shang-Chi is just a uniquely proficient martial artist. Then there's DC's Mister Terrific—powerless, but as his name not-so-subtly suggests, is terrific at just about everything.

Then there are the superheroes who have no powers themselves, but utilize a device of some kind that allows them to do superhuman things. Iron Man is the most famous example—he's just a guy in a suit. (Sure, there was a story in the comics recently where part of the suit was actually inside his body, and he could control it with his mind, but that's over now.) Green Lantern is another—an average dude without his power ring, but nearly limitless in power with it on.

by Albert Ching

What's the Most Expensive Movie Ever Made?

In Hollywood, as in life, it seems you get what you pay for. So when James Cameron convinced 20th Century Fox to finance his ambitious 3-D science fiction epic *Avatar*, the studio executives surely had high hopes for what the Oscar-winning filmmaker would deliver. But perhaps they were also more than a little nervous, and with good reason.

The production budget for *Avatar* was a reported $280 million, making it the most expensive movie of all time, according to *Vanity Fair Magazine*. But as astronomical as that dollar figure is, it may actually have lowballed the picture's true cost.

Factor in worldwide marketing and print costs as the *New York Times* did, and the true price tag of Cameron's trip to Pandora may actually be closer to $500 million. Most movie budget estimates don't factor in a film's marketing costs, even though those expenses can often end up doubling a movie's budget.

It turned out to be a bargain. *Avatar* not only earned back its mammoth budget, it did so with ease. Thanks in part to repeat viewings and especially the higher priced 3-D screenings, *Avatar* became the all-time box-office champ with more

> *AVATAR* MAY HAVE COST THE MOST TO MAKE, BUT THANKS IN PART TO REPEAT VIEWINGS & THE HIGHER PRICED 3-D SCREENINGS, *AVATAR* BECAME THE ALL-TIME BOX-OFFICE CHAMP WITH MORE THAN $2.7 BILLION. THAT'S RIGHT, BILLION IN TICKET SALES, ACCORDING TO THE INDUSTRY TRACKING WEBSITE *BOX OFFICE MOJO.* THE MOVIE WAS ALSO NOMINATED FOR NINE ACADEMY AWARDS AND WON THREE.

than $2.7 billion—that's right, billion—in ticket sales, according to the industry tracking website *Box Office Mojo*. It was also nominated for nine Academy Awards and won three.

What movie did *Avatar* topple from the all-time No. 1 spot? It sunk *Titanic*, another high-priced Cameron epic that earned $1.8 billion, to No. 2.

It should be noted that *Box Office Mojo* cites Disney's *Pirates of the Caribbean: At World's End* as the most expensive film ever, with a price tag of $300 million. However, that third chapter in the *Pirates* movies was shot simultaneously with the second movie of the franchise, *Pirates of the Caribbean: Dead Man's Chest*, so it could be next to impossible to figure out exactly how much each of those movies cost.

James Cameron has proven to be one of the most reliable earners in the industry, with blockbusters such as *Aliens, True Lies* and *Terminator 2: Judgment Day*.

If there's one thing we know about James Cameron, it's that no matter how big the budget, his movies are money in the bank.

by Michael Avila

Who's the Highest Paid Actor?

Trying to determine the highest paid actor in Hollywood is a dicey proposition. Actors' contracts are famous for their complex incentives, and a comparison is made all the more difficult by the notoriously pliable financial agreements of the movie industry. And let's face it, what rich guy likes to open up his checkbook to show you his current balance?

We also have to take into account that many stars, including Will Smith, Tom Hanks, Tyler Perry, Adam Sandler and Ben Stiller, do other well-paying jobs such as producing, writing and directing. But for now, we'll focus on acting earnings only.

According to *Vanity Fair* magazine, the highest paid actor in 2009 was *Harry Potter* star Daniel Radcliffe, with $41 million in earnings. The face of the biggest franchise in movie history was reportedly paid $20 million for each of the last two *Potter* films.

Stiller came in second place, with $37 million for his work in the *Meet the Parents* sequel *Little Fockers*, as well as his starring roles in *Greenberg*, *Night at the Museum: Battle of the Smithsonian*, and the animated *Madagascar: Escape 2 Africa*.

Hanks pocketed $36 million each for his acting role in *Angels & Demons* and his voice-over work in *Toy Story 3*.

HARRISON FORD TOOK HOME $65 MILLION FOR PUTTING ON THE FEDORA AGAIN IN 2008 FOR *INDIANA JONES AND THE KINGDOM OF THE CRYSTAL SKULL*. AND KEANU REEVES BLEW THAT OUT OF THE WATER BY REPORTEDLY EARNING $194 MILLION FROM THE *MATRIX* TRILOGY.

But those three actors combined didn't earn as much as Hollywood's top dollar man in 2009—director Michael Bay. He reportedly earned $125 million from producing and directing *Transformers: Revenge of the Fallen*, including his share of the DVD and toy revenue for that movie franchise.

Johnny Depp earned as much as $56 million to reprise his role as Captain Jack Sparrow in *Pirates of the Caribbean 4*.

But as stratospheric as that number is, it's far from an all-time record.

Harrison Ford took home $65 million for putting on the fedora again in 2008 for *Indiana Jones and the Kingdom of the Crystal Skull*.

And Keanu Reeves blew that out of the water by reportedly earning $194 million from the *Matrix* trilogy. Why so much? The actor known for playing air-headed roles early in his career was smart enough to cut a deal guaranteeing him a piece of the profits from that enormously popular film series.

by Michael Avila

What TV Shows Have Aired the Most Original Episodes?

he Simpsons is the longest-running American prime-time series, consistently running a season each year since its debut on Dec. 17, 1989, but while it may be the longest running, the title of most original episodes goes to a different show—*Gunsmoke*.

Gone are the days when shows would get a season or two to find their audience, like *Cheers* and *Seinfeld* did. The high costs of producing network television means that series run with fewer episodes. Most scripted programs today produce no more than 22 episodes per season. It wasn't uncommon for older shows like *Gunsmoke* and *Lassie* to churn out more than 30 episodes a season.

The following are the five American prime-time scripted TV series that produced the most episodes:

1. Gunsmoke (1955-75): 635 episodes. This classic Western's prodigious output will likely never be matched. James Arness starred as Marshall Matt Dillon in all 20 seasons, another industry record. The show was TV's top-rated show from 1957 to 1961 and never finished out of the Nielsen Top 30.

THE HIGH COSTS OF PRODUCING NETWORK TELEVISION MEANS THAT SERIES RUN WITH FEWER EPISODES. MOST SCRIPTED PROGRAMS TODAY PRODUCE NO MORE THAN 22 EPISODES PER SEASON. IT WASN'T UNCOMMON FOR OLDER SHOWS LIKE *GUNSMOKE* AND *LASSIE* TO CHURN OUT MORE THAN 30 EPISODES A SEASON.

The show's original outdoor sets in Simi Valley, Calif., were later used on another long-running show, *Little House on the Prairie*.

2. Lassie (1954-73): 588 episodes. One of the first true crossover stars, *Lassie* began as a movie star, appearing in seven films for MGM before moving on to small-screen stardom. *Lassie* aired on CBS for its first 17 seasons and won two Emmys for its family-friendly messages.

Six different dogs portrayed Lassie, with Baby lasting the longest, from 1960 to 1966.

3. The Simpsons (1989-present): 463 episodes. Matt Groening's beloved animated series *The Simpsons* completed its 21st season in 2010, making it the longest-running American prime-time series.

The Simpsons has won 25 Emmys and a Peabody Award, and was named the 20th Century's Best TV Show by *Time Magazine*. Writer John Swartzwelder has written the most *Simpsons* episodes, 60 in all.

4. Law & Order (1990-2010): 455 episodes. The legal show was a cornerstone of NBC's prime-time lineup for two decades, but it was supposed to debut on Fox. However, Fox executives didn't feel it was a good fit for the network of *Married with Children* and *In Living Color*, so they passed.

The show, which ran for 21 seasons, inspired four spin-offs under the *Law & Order* banner, *Criminal Intent, Special Victims Unit, Trial By Jury* and *Law & Order: Los Angeles*.

5. The Adventures of Ozzie & Harriet (1952-1966): 435 episodes. The quintessential, all-American family sitcom, *Ozzie & Harriet* started out as a radio program. After 402 episodes, it moved to television.

Ozzie and Harriet Nelson, along with their real children David and Ricky, became instant stars. Ricky, in particular, became one of the first teen idols of the TV generation. *The Adventures of Ozzie & Harriet* aired in black and white for all but its 14th and final season.

by Michael Avila

What Was the First Feature-Length Computer Animated Film?

oy Story 3, which was the highest grossing movie of 2010, was the first film in the *Toy Story* franchise to be screened in 3-D. But 3-D isn't the first "first" for its main characters, Woody and Buzz Lightyear.

The bickering buddies were part of another watershed moment in 1995, when *Toy Story* became the first feature-length computer-animated movie.

The entire movie was created with computer-generated imagery (CGI). It marked a huge departure from the longtime industry animation standard of animated films being made from hand-drawn pictures.

The *Toy Story* movie franchise not only launched Pixar as a creative powerhouse, but it marked the arrival of an entirely new way of making animated movies.

CGI, which was first used as a visual effects tool in the 1973 live-action film *Westworld*, has now become the dominant tool in animation. Because of the speed and limitless possibilities provided by modern-day computing power, computer animation is credited with revolutionizing live-action visual effects. And with animated movies, it has expanded the potential of the medium to the point that the impossible has become possible.

Toy Story (1995) was the first full-length movie that was created entirely with computer-generated imagery (CGI). It marked a huge departure from the longtime industry animation standard of animated films being made from hand-drawn pictures.

How CGI Became the Standard. Before CGI came along, animated films were hand-drawn masterworks. Walt Disney basically invented the animated movie genre, and with his legendary group of animators—his Nine Old Men—turned out classics such as *Snow White and the Seven Dwarfs*, *Lady and the Tramp* and *Pinocchio*.

And when feature-film animation experienced its rebirth in 1989, it was thanks to *The Little Mermaid's* hand-drawn, two-dimensional imagery. But then, *Toy Story* came along six years later and essentially put a stake through the heart of traditional animation. Now, 3-D computer-generated animation is standard issue.

There are still those who believe in the power and effectiveness of traditional, 2-D animation. Perhaps ironically, the loudest voice belongs to John Lasseter, the Chief Creative Officer at Pixar and Disney Animated Studios.

An avowed fan of old-school animation, he spearheaded the 2009 release of The *Princess and the Frog*, a film that marked a return to the classic Disney style of animation. But while the film was a solid critical and commercial success, it didn't come close to reaching the level of acclaim and box-office appeal that Pixar's CGI-created *Up* experienced that year.

We can thank the *Toy Story* crew for setting the bar so high.

by Michael Avila

What Is the Most Successful Zombie Movie Ever?

he most successful zombie movie ever is *Zombieland*. The 2009 horror comedy starring Jesse Eisenberg and Woody Harrelson as survivors trying to escape a zombie-filled landscape earned $75 million at the box office, according to the industry-tracking site *Box Office Mojo*.

However, a look at the zombie genre beyond the box office totals reveals that the most successful zombie movie ever, in terms of both profit and cultural impact, is George A. Romero's 1968 horror classic *Night of the Living Dead*.

Romero has crafted a career out of his fascination with zombies. The writer-director's sixth film about the slow moving, flesh-eating undead, *Survival of the Dead*, hit theaters May 28, 2010. But Romero will be hard-pressed to top his greatest zombie success, which was also his first.

Night of the Living Dead influenced every zombie movie to follow in its slow-moving path, according to Baylor University assistant professor and zombie authority James Kendrick. He credits the movie with inventing the now-standard genre template of a zombie as a reanimated corpse with a taste for human flesh. Before then, zombies in movies were typically people in a trance or under the control of someone else.

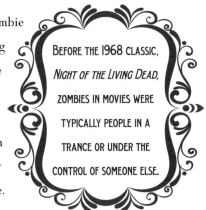

BEFORE THE 1968 CLASSIC, *NIGHT OF THE LIVING DEAD,* ZOMBIES IN MOVIES WERE TYPICALLY PEOPLE IN A TRANCE OR UNDER THE CONTROL OF SOMEONE ELSE.

"Thus, every movie since 1968 that features reanimated corpses running amok owes something to Romero's black and white masterpiece," says Kendrick, who has written several books on zombies and teaches a course on zombie films.

The movie also changed attitudes toward horror movies.

"Romero's film helped to revive the horror genre in the U.S., which had largely sunk into parody in the 1950s, with all the *Abbott and Costello Meets ...* movies," Kendrick says. He also points out that the word "zombie" is never uttered in *Night of the Living Dead*.

Aside from the fact that it basically launched its own sub-genre of horror, *Night of the Living Dead* is one the most profitable zombie films in history. The movie was made on a budget of just $114,000, and it has earned more than $30 million worldwide when the totals from its re-releases over the years are included.

Despite the film's enormous success, Romero and the film's producers didn't earn much of a windfall. Due to an oversight by the distributor, who left the copyright notice off the film, the movie lapsed into the public domain, so it's available to view or legally download for free from many websites including YouTube.

Perhaps the greatest indicator of the success of *Night of the Living Dead* is the subsequent good fortune of the horror film genre as a whole.

Along with Hitchcock's *Psycho* (1960), *Night of the Living Dead* made horror horrific again, mostly by taking the genre seriously and using it to sociopolitical ends, says Kendrick, explaining that the film served as a metaphor for the social issues of the time.

It seems the Library of Congress agrees. In 1999, it selected Romero's landmark picture for preservation in the National Film Registry, citing its cultural significance.

by Michael Avila

Who Has Starred in Prime-Time TV Shows in Three Different Decades?

f success in television was measured by longevity, then perhaps relative newcomers like John Krasinski of *The Office* and Adrian Grenier of *Entourage* would do well to study up on the careers of Bill Cosby, Michael Landon and Lee Majors.

Each of these three achieved the near impossible: They starred in not one, not two, but three hit prime-time TV series, in three separate decades.

Landon was the first to reach stardom. In the classic western *Bonanza*, he played Little Joe Cartwright. *Bonanza* was the most popular TV series of the 1960s and ran for 14 seasons, from 1959 to 1973.

One year after *Bonanza* was cancelled, Landon created one of the most popular family shows of the 1970s, *Little House on the Prairie*, which ran from 1974 to 1983. He then moved on to *Highway to Heaven*, which ran for five seasons from 1984 to 1989. All together, Landon spent 30 family-friendly years on television.

Bill Cosby broke the race barrier in 1965 when he became the first black actor to co-star in a TV drama. The hit *I Spy* ran for three seasons, and Cosby won three Emmy Awards for his work.

Then, after several failed series, Cosby found his greatest success in 1984 with *The Cosby Show*. One of only two sitcoms to top television's Nielsen ratings five years in a row, *The Cosby Show* is credited with saving the sitcom as a viable format. Cosby scored another, albeit more modest, sitcom hit with *Cosby*, which debuted in 1996 and aired for four seasons.

If you count the 1970s animated Saturday morning kids show, *Fat Albert and the Cosby Kids*, then Cosby actually managed to score TV hits in four separate decades. He was the voice of several of the show's characters.

The final member of this exclusive club, Lee Majors, broke through playing Heath Barkley in the western *Big Valley*, which ran from 1965-1969. Then, in 1974, Majors scored his most memorable role as Col. Steve Austin in the science-fiction action hit The *Six Million Dollar Man*. The show, which lasted five seasons, made Majors an icon, complete with an action figure and lunchbox.

> MICHAEL LANDON STARRED AS JOE CARTWRIGHT IN THE 1960S CLASSIC TV SHOW *BONANZA*, AS CHARLES INGALLS IN *LITTLE HOUSE ON THE PRAIRIE* IN THE 70S, & AS JONATHAN SMITH OF *HIGHWAY TO HEAVEN* IN THE 1980S. LANDON, WHO TRAGICALLY DIED OF CANCER IN 1991 AT AGE 54, WAS ONE OF ONLY A HANDFUL OF ACTORS WHO HAVE ACCOMPLISHED THE FEAT OF STARRING IN PRIME-TIME TV SHOWS IN THREE DIFFERENT DECADES.

Majors overcame the stigma of being the Bionic Man by poking fun at his action hero image. He played a stuntman/bounty hunter in his next hit series, *The Fall Guy*, which aired through the mid-1980s. The role of Colt Seavers allowed Majors to show off his comedic side, as well as sing the show's memorable theme song.

by Michael Avila

Chapter 7
Money

Reading the financial section of a newspaper will leave you thinking that money, not love, keeps the world going round. The present recession that our global economy has been experiencing has gotten more of us paying attention to business news such as the daily New York Stock Exchange's closing bell figures, unemployment rates, and tax-related legislation. We hope the following money-related trivia will inform but also lift your spirits.

Which Single Piece of Currency Is Worth the Most?

 he rare $10,000 bill is the most valuable U.S. currency now in circulation.

The Treasury stopped printing it, along with the $500, $1,000 and $5,000 denominations, during World War II, and all such bills stopped being printed on July 14, 1969. Today, Federal Reserve Banks destroy these notes when they receive them, but they remain legal tender while in circulation according to the U.S. Department of the Treasury.

The $10,000 bill is also the most valuable circulating global currency, according to Roberto Cacciamani, former director of the International Bank Note Society. Tied for second place are the 10,000 SGD (Singapore dollar) note and the 10,000 BND (Brunei dollar) note, each equal to around $7,400, according to rates provided by Citibank N.A.

Runners-up include the 500 LVL (Latvian lats) and 1,000 CHF (Swiss franc) notes, each worth around $1,000.

Higher denominations exist as limited-edition commemorative notes issued to honor important persons or events, but because they are not circulating, they are not considered currency, according to Cacciamani.

If Thailand's 500,000-baht commemorative note were a circulating currency, it would take the prize as the most valuable piece of legal tender in the world—its value is about $15,600.

> If Thailand's 500,000-baht commemorative note were a circulating currency, it would take the prize as the most valuable piece of legal tender in the world its value is about $15,600.

Along similar lines, the most valuable U.S. note ever produced was the $100,000 gold certificate, only 42,000 of which were printed during their Dec. 18, 1934, through Jan. 9, 1935, run.

But the certificates were never in public circulation—the Treasury Department issued them solely to Federal Reserve Banks, which used them only for transactions with one another. This practice continued until the early 1960s, when the government destroyed all but a few, which are now held by the Federal Reserve Bank of San Francisco, the Bureau of Engraving and Printing and the Smithsonian Institute.

by Nicholas Gerbis

What Are the Most Bizarre Luxury Taxes?

 uxury taxes, the mercurial fines that are tacked onto extravagant items like fancy cars and expensive jewelry, are a way to force those who can afford to buy these big-ticket items to contribute to society.

This form of taxation is placed on products that are not considered essential and is aimed at making the wealthy pay more for their lavish spending habits. A way to raise state revenue, luxury taxes can be put on anything from designer clothes to real estate transactions. Luxury taxes are rarely national, and they vary from state to state.

"In the United States, the only mass luxury tax was the tax on automobiles costing more than 40,000 dollars, and that expired in 2002," says Paul Zane Pilzer, economist and author of *The Next Millionaires*. "It didn't apply to trucks or SUVs and was a nuisance."

Other luxury taxes have met a similar end. For example, when drafting the 2009-2010 state budget, New York state legislators wanted to include an additional 5 percent luxury tax on jewelry, watches and furs that cost more than $20,000. The proposed luxury tax would have also been applied to aircraft costing more than $500,000, yachts costing more than $200,000 and cars costing more than $60,000. However, this luxury tax was struck down.

Often adjusted based on the state of the economy and inflation, luxury taxes are not to be confused with sin taxes, which are applied by the government as a way to discourage the use of products and services that could pose a risk to someone's health, such as alcohol and cigarettes. In the United States, Puritan colonists created the earliest sin taxes, according to the IRS.

"Sin taxes are designed to modify human behavior and/or tax people for the cost to society of their 'sin,' like smoking, drinking, or polluting." Pilzer tells *Life's Little Mysteries*. "Sin taxes are generally very effective in fairly charging people for their bad behavior but have had little success in actually modifying behavior."

Both sin and luxury taxes have been around for hundreds of years, and throughout history, there have been some pretty bizarre ones. The following are a few.

Currently Alabama has a tax tacked onto the price of a deck of cards—10 cents for a deck containing "no more than 54 cards." The state also taxes stores for selling the cards with "an annual license tax of $3 and a fee of $1," according to the Alabama Department of Revenue.

> LUXURY TAXES ARE PLACED ON PRODUCTS THAT ARE NOT CONSIDERED ESSENTIAL AND ARE AIMED AT MAKING THE WEALTHY PAY MORE FOR THEIR LAVISH SPENDING HABITS. A WAY TO RAISE STATE REVENUE, LUXURY TAXES CAN BE PUT ON ANYTHING FROM DESIGNER CLOTHES TO REAL ESTATE TRANSACTIONS.

In September 2009, Illinois decided to tax candy at a higher rate than other food. Similarly, Gov. David A. Paterson (NY) proposed tax on sugary sodas in 2010, which would have added a penny-an-ounce tax on soda and other sweet drinks. The proposed tax was dropped from the state revenue bill.

In 2005, the Canadian Parliament proposed bills that aimed to put an excise tax, of which sin taxes are considered to be one form, on prostitution.

Winners of the Nobel and Pulitzer Prizes must pay a special tax to the IRS. "If you were awarded a prize in recognition of accomplishments in religious, charitable, scientific, artistic, educational, literary, or civic fields, you generally must include the value of the prize in your income," according to the IRS's website.

Peter the Great, Tsar of Russia during the late 17th and early 18th centuries, hated beards so much that he required all men except peasants and priests to pay him a yearly tax for sporting a beard. Those who paid the tax were also forced to wear a medal proclaiming, "Beards are a ridiculous ornament," says Diane Stanley in her book, *Peter the Great*.

In the 14th century, England taxed its citizens for simply being alive. This tax was increased to triple its original amount, until the people finally protested the outrageous tax during what is now known as the Peasants' Revolt of 1381.

by Remy Melina

Why Is it Called 'Wall Street'?

all Street—an actual street by that name—is located in Lower Manhattan in New York City. The street acts as the epicenter of the city's Financial District.

The name of the street originates from an actual wall that was built in the 17th century by the Dutch, who were living in what was then called New Amsterdam. The 12-foot (4 m) wall was built to protect the Dutch against attacks from pirates and various Native American tribes, and to keep other potential dangers out of the establishment.

The area near the wall became known as Wall Street. Because of its prime location— running the width of Manhattan between the East River and the Hudson River—the road developed into one of the busiest trading areas in the entire city. Later, in 1699, the wall was dismantled by the British colonial government, but the name of the street stuck.

The financial industry got its official start on Wall Street on May 17, 1792. On that day, New York's first official stock exchange was established by the signing of the Buttonwood Agreement. The agreement, so-called because it was signed under a buttonwood tree around which early traders and speculators had previously gathered to trade informally, gave birth to what is now the modern-day New York Stock Exchange (NYSE).

THE NAME ORIGINATES FROM AN ACTUAL WALL THAT WAS BUILT IN THE 17TH CENTURY BY THE DUTCH, WHO WERE LIVING IN WHAT WAS THEN CALLED NEW AMSTERDAM. THE 12-FOOT (4 M) WALL WAS BUILT TO PROTECT THE DUTCH AGAINST ATTACKS FROM PIRATES & VARIOUS NATIVE AMERICAN TRIBES, & TO KEEP OTHER POTENTIAL DANGERS OUT OF THE ESTABLISHMENT.

Events on Wall Street including the huge losses of large banks due to over-investing in derivative markets and the collapse of the U.S. real estate market in recent years were the cause of the recession that has rocked the global economy.

Today, "Wall Street" is used to describe the country's financial sector. Since the start of the latest economic recession, in some circles, the term "Wall Street" has become a metaphor for corporate greed and financial mismanagement.

by Denise Chow

When Are We in a Recession?

o the average American, it might seem ludicrous to suggest that the United States is not in a recession right now. But economists' fuzzy definition of the term makes it hard to say when a recession actually starts until we're well into one.

You might hear, for example, that a recession occurs when gross domestic product (GDP) growth is negative for two or more consecutive quarters. But that's not an adequate measure, most economists agree.

The National Bureau of Economic Research (NBER), a non-profit group that includes economic researchers and professors from all over the country, has a somewhat formal definition that is often cited, says Michael Bernstein, provost and professor of economics and history at Tulane University.

"NBER would define a recession as a significant decline in economic activity that spreads across the economy and that lasts more than a few months," Bernstein says. "Normally it would be visible in data on real income, employment, industrial output, sales, Gross Domestic Product (GDP), that sort of thing."

As for duration, recessions can last for those "few months" or up to about two years. The factors that predict a recession also are not entirely simple.

Potential Predictors. The stock markets have received a lot of attention during the recent economic decline, but Bernstein said that economists have found that stock market indicators alone aren't very good predictors of recessions.

"As much as we try, we cannot demonstrate a close statistical relationship between how the stock market moves and how the so-called business cycle moves. Sometimes they're linked, sometimes not," he tells *LiveScience*, a sister online magazine to *Life's Little Mysteries*.

The stock market can certainly fall in relation to a recession though. Stock market fluctuations are a result of traders' perceptions regarding the health of national banks and publicly traded corporations

The terms "bear market" and "bull market" also have nothing to do with whether or not the economy is in a recession. They're simply colloquial expressions: the market is bearish when people are nervous about buying and they start selling off shares, whereas in a bullish market people take more risks and are buying more.

One factor that is a better predictor of a recession is the real estate market, Bernstein says, as they have been in the present recession. When houses are being built, jobs are created and production in construction-related industries goes up, but when real estate sales stagnate, related jobs and production revenue are lost. Similarly, refinancing on homes frees up money that homeowners can spend on other things, but when homes drop in value, there's no money to spend.

"As much as we try, we cannot demonstrate a close statistical relationship between how the stock market moves and how the so-called business cycle moves. Sometimes they're linked, sometimes not," says Michael Bernstein, provost and professor of economics and history at Tulane University.

Recessions and Depressions Past. The last recession the country faced was nearly a decade ago when the "dot-com" bubble burst, taking under countless companies and sending many to the unemployment line. But that downturn was mild compared to the current recession, which is probably more comparable to the U.S. recession of the late 1980s.

"The last big slide was in 1987, when the stock market went down by about 20 percent, and the economy went into the toilet for about five years," Bernstein says.

Of course, none of the 10 recessions since 1945 that the NBER recognizes compare to the magnitude of the Great Depression.

Though the Great Depression lasted for about a decade, it isn't necessarily longevity that turns a recession into a depression. It's the depth of the crisis. The 1930s saw a 25 to 30 percent drop in GDP, and unemployment went up to 25 percent.

For comparison, the national unemployment rate was about 10 percent in the last two quarters of 2010. In 2008, real GDP (the output of goods and services by sectors in the United States) rose by 2.8 percent from the first quarter to the second quarter, according to the Bureau of Economic Analysis; it rose by 0.9 percent in the first quarter of 2010.

And there are, of course, some financial safeguards in place since the Great Depression, such as depositor insurance. These safeguards have kept subsequent economic crises from reaching the same severe proportions, though they don't keep any recession from being downright dismal.

by Andrea Thompson

What Exactly Is Social Security? (And How Much Money Do You Get?)

n the United States, "social security" usually refers to the government's social insurance program, which provides payments to disabled people, retired workers and their spouses and families. This insurance is officially called the Old-Age, Survivors and Disability Insurance (OASDI) program.

Social security is funded by taxing workers' pay through the Federal Insurance Contributions Act tax, commonly called FICA. In 2010, the social security tax rate was 6.2 percent on earnings up to $106,800. Any income earned above that amount was not subject to the tax.

How Did Social Security Get Started? OASDI was put into place by the Social Security Act, signed by President Franklin Roosevelt on Aug. 14, 1935, as a way to protect the elderly from poverty and ease the effects of unemployment. Originally, the act only subjected some jobs to paying the tax, and only people in those jobs could receive benefits.

Today, most work—even self-employment—is subject to and benefits from social security. The original program also didn't include disability insurance, or benefits for a surviving family. These provisions were added later.

According to the Social Security Administration (SSA), the first social security taxes were collected in 1937, and the first regular payments were made to a retired woman named Ida Mae Fuller in 1940. Fuller received $22.40 monthly.

OASDI paid a total of $35 million in benefits in 1940. By 2008, total social security payments rose to more than $500 billion yearly, according to the SSA.

How Much Do You Get? To receive social security, a worker must have worked at least 10 years, or collected 40 credits in the program's credit system, according to the SSA. Workers receive a credit for every $1,120 they earn, up to 4 credits per year.

To receive disability benefits, a person must suffer a disability that both meets the system's criteria and prevents them from working. Covered disabilities include a range of injuries and illnesses, such as a limb amputation and diseases of the immune system.

> ACCORDING TO THE SOCIAL SECURITY ADMINISTRATION, THE FIRST SOCIAL SECURITY TAXES WERE COLLECTED IN 1937, AND THE FIRST REGULAR PAYMENTS WERE MADE TO A RETIRED WOMAN NAMED IDA MAE FULLER IN 1940. FULLER RECEIVED $22.40 MONTHLY.

The official retirement age at which you can receive full benefits is 66. Workers can retire as early as 62, but they receive reduced benefits, according to the SSA. The longer you continue working after age 65, the more your monthly payout will be.

The amount of money you receive is based on the average of your 35 highest-paid years, and it is adjusted for inflation in the cost of living over your lifetime. Workers who worked more years, or had a higher salary and higher tax payments into the system, receive higher payments when they become eligible. As of 2010, the average monthly benefit is about $1,050 according to the AARP.

In most years of the OASDI program, payments contributed into the system by working people have equaled or exceeded payments out. But with the large numbers of baby boomers entering retirement and a historical decline in birthrates reducing the number of workers paying in, this balance is not expected to continue, according to projections.

People of all political ideologies have proposed ways to fix the imbalance—they range from privatizing all or part of the system to raising social security taxes on higher incomes.

by Molika Ashford

Which U.S. Cities Have the Most Millionaires?

oasting the highest number of millionaires of any U.S. city, New York City should perhaps change its nickname from "The Big Apple" to "The Golden Apple."

The New York metropolitan area has 650,000 high-net worth individuals (HNWIs), or people with $1 million or more in investible assets (which excludes their primary residence, collectibles, consumables and consumer durables), according to the 2010 Metro Wealth Index. The index, constructed by the Paris-based consulting firm Capgemini, annually tracks affluent households in hundreds of cities nationwide.

According to the numbers, New York City continues to top the index and has more high net worth individuals than the next top three cities—Los Angeles, Chicago and Washington, D.C.—combined.

Interestingly, the index shows that despite the recession, the number of HNWIs in the 10 cities that have the most of them increased by 17.5 percent from 2008 to 2009, the highest growth rate in the last four years. The number of HNWIs in New York City grew by 18.7 percent during that time.

How did the Empire City manage to have such a millionaire boom in the midst of these dreary economic conditions?

The use of U.S. taxpayers' money to fund bank bailouts certainly helped those on Wall Street, Cornell University professor of economics Robert H. Frank noted in a blog post about the 2010 index in the *Wall Street Journal*, adding that finance, technology and oil still remain the main sources of wealth in the United States.

by Remy Melina

2010 U.S. METRO WEALTH INDEX	
NEW YORK	667,200 (+18.7%)
LOS ANGELES	235,800 (+13.3%)
CHICAGO	198,100 (+15.1%)
WASHINGTON D.C.	152,400 (+19.3%)
SAN FRANCISCO	138,300 (+14.5%)
PHILADELPHIA	104,100 (+20.1%)
BOSTON	102,300 (+14.4%)
DETROIT	89,100 (+12.1%)
HOUSTON	88,200 (+28.9%)
SAN JOSE	86,500 (+24.5%)

Chapter 8
Sports

There are a number of sports throughout the world, each with their own group of fans. Sports such as football, basketball, baseball and soccer provide the groundwork of mini-cultures and give us heroes to admire and emulate. Most sports as we know them have existed for only about the last century, each with fascinating stories about how they evolved and came to be. In this chapter, we provide answers about sports' stats and its rich traditions.

Why Is it Called the World Series?

n 1903, Barney Dreyfuss, owner of the Pittsburgh Pirates, sent a letter to the owner of the Boston Americans, now known as the Boston Red Sox, challenging the team to "a World's Championship Series."

That season, the Pirates had the best record in the National League, and the Red Sox ranked No. 1 in the American League. Boston won that year's best-of-nine series, 5 games to 3. The series has since been shortened to seven games.

The World's Championship Series—whose name was later shortened to World Series— has been played every year since, except 1904 and 1994.

"In 1904, the New York Giants refused to play the Red Sox," says Freddy Berowski, a research associate at the National Baseball Hall of Fame and Museum in Cooperstown, N.Y. "The leagues stepped in the following year to officially make the World Series an annual event. In 1994, the baseball strike prevented the playing of the World Series."

> THE WORLD'S CHAMPIONSHIP SERIES, WHOSE NAME WAS LATER SHORTENED TO WORLD SERIES, HAS BEEN PLAYED EVERY YEAR SINCE 1903, EXCEPT 1904 AND 1994.

The term "World Series" first appeared in 1917 in the *Spalding Guides*, guides to the game published by the Spalding Athletic Company in the late 19th and early 20th centuries. The *Sporting News* picked up the guides in 1964, according to the *Dickson Baseball Dictionary*.

The term "World Series" was used on the Cleveland scorecard in 1920 and the Washington scorecard in 1924.

"A popular myth is that the World Series was named for the *New York World Telegram*," says Berowski. Although the newspaper reported the game's results, Barney Dreyfuss deserves credit for naming the series.

by Corey Binns

Are the Chicago Cubs Really Cursed?

sk most fans of the Cubbies the question, "Are the Chicago Cubs really cursed?" and a good number will shout out, "YES!"

Can you blame them? The Cubs haven't won a World Series in 102 years. They're the lovable losers, a team whose championship futility has become as much a part of the franchise's identity as the ivy climbing the walls of the outfield at Wrigley Field.

The 2010 Cubs failed to make the playoffs, ensuring another year without a World Series appearance, and guaranteeing that the legendary Curse of the Billy Goat endures for at least one more season.

What, you don't know about the Cubbies' curse?

The Curse Is Cast. Legend has it that the so-called curse has its origins in the 1945 World Series. According to Mickey Bradley, co-author of *Haunted Baseball*, a book about the spooky relationship between baseball and the paranormal, it all began on Oct. 6, 1945, at Wrigley Field during Game 4 of the Fall Classic.

That day, Billy Sianis, owner of the nearby Billy Goat Tavern, attended the game with his pet goat. At first, he was refused entry, according to Bradley and other accounts, but because he had a ticket for the goat, the ushers relented.

Then it rained. The odor from the soggy animal began getting the "goat" of nearby fans, and security booted Sianis and the goat.

Angered over what he felt was shabby treatment, Sianis reportedly cursed the Cubs outside the stadium. In his book, *Da Curse of the Billy Goat, The Cubs, Pennant Races, and Curses,* Author Steve Gatto writes that Sianis' family insists the tavern owner issued his curse via telegram to the team's owner, P.K. Wrigley, declaring that, "You are going to lose this World Series.... You are never going to win the World Series again because you insulted my goat."

The Cubs haven't been back to the World Series since. The Curse of the Billy Goat has become an urban legend rivaling that of the alligators in the New York City sewers and Bigfoot. But the question remains: Are the Cubs really cursed? It may depend on one's perspective.

> THE CURSE OF THE BILLY GOAT HAS BECOME AN URBAN LEGEND RIVALING THAT OF THE ALLIGATORS IN THE NEW YORK CITY SEWERS & BIGFOOT. BUT THE QUESTION REMAINS: ARE THE CUBS REALLY CURSED? IT MAY DEPEND ON ONE'S PERSPECTIVE.

"Curses are as powerful as people's belief in them," Bradley said. If players start believing such circumstances as a curse are preventing them from achieving success, "it can become a self-fulfilling prophecy."

Strange Happenings. It's easy to overlook the injuries, bad player signings, sub-par pitching and erratic defense that often determine whether a team wins or loses in baseball. Sometimes you want to blame extraneous factors for the rotten luck. Why not blame a Billy Goat?

It's also hard to argue with more than a century's worth of losing, often in circumstances that can challenge even the most disbelieving fan's resolve. The evidence certainly supports those who believe the Sianis curse is real.

In 1969, a promising season ended with a late-season collapse that longtime Cubs fans blame on a September game at Shea Stadium. In that game, a black cat ran onto the field and circled the Cubs' third baseman Ron Santo. The Cubs lost that game to the Mets and eventually collapsed and missed the playoffs.

In 1984, the Cubs won their first title of any kind since 1945 when they captured the National League (NL) Eastern Division. Needing just one win in the NL Championship Series over the San Diego Padres to return to the World Series, the Cubs proceeded to lose three straight games. The most crushing moment: First baseman Leon Durham's 7th-inning error in the deciding Game 5.

But it was the heartbreak of 2003 that supporters of the curse point to as Exhibit A in their case.

That was the year the Cubs, up 3 games to 2 and just five outs away from returning to the World Series for the first time in 58 years, added the "Steve Bartman incident" to their history of misery.

Bartman, a Cubs fan now-infamously sat in Aisle 4, Row 8, Seat 113 at Wrigley Field for Game 6 of the National League Championship Series, and prevented Cubs outfielder Moises Alou from most likely catching a foul ball that drifted just over the outfield wall when he did what so many fans do at the ballpark: try to grab a souvenir foul ball.

That would have been the second out of the inning. Alas, the inning continued and the Marlins erupted for eight runs, to rally and win. Florida won Game 7 and went on to win the World Series that year.

Steve Bartman was ostracized, even threatened, for what some fans felt was an inexcusable act. His unfortunate action that night continues to resonate seven years later; ESPN even scheduled to produce a documentary called *Steve Bartman: Catching Hell*, but they postponed it in October 2010.

"It's a natural human compulsion to look for explanations and patterns in odd occurrences," Bradley says. "The team has not been to the World Series since Sianis 'cursed' them; they have not won a World Series in more than 100 years."

Some Cubs fans may also put stock in the curse because it reaffirms their support of their ballclub. Being a fan of a team known for pulling defeat from the jaws of victory takes a certain amount of character. For the Cubs faithful, believing in the curse is like a badge of honor.

As someone told Bradley, "Anyone can win the World Series, but it takes a special team to lose for 100 years!"

Spoken like a true fan.

by Michael Avila

Which Boxer Has Won the Most Championship Belts?

I t used to be so simple in boxing: To be the man, you had to beat the man. There were eight weight classes, and if you beat the champ in a weight class, you became the new champ. A proliferation of weight classes and belt-bestowing regulatory bodies has since complicated the matter, making it almost impossible to determine who the real champ is, and who has won the most championships.

Nominally, the winner of the most championships is either Roy Jones Jr., who won 12 belts in four different weight classes, or Manny Pacquiao, who has won 12 belts in eight different weight classes. Because the legitimacy of some of those belts remains in question, however, those totals don't tell the whole story, says Tim Starks, boxing journalist and author of the blog Queensberry-rules.com.

"The thing about these belts is that almost anyone can win one. They practically give them out as prizes in Cracker Jack boxes," Starks tells *Life's Little Mysteries*. "I don't know the record for most belts won overall. Boxers win and lose belts all the time, and that makes it so you can say 'twelve-time world champion' or whatever. It's largely meaningless."

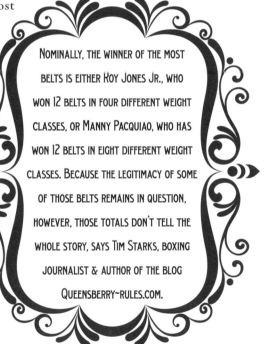

NOMINALLY, THE WINNER OF THE MOST BELTS IS EITHER ROY JONES JR., WHO WON 12 BELTS IN FOUR DIFFERENT WEIGHT CLASSES, OR MANNY PACQUIAO, WHO HAS WON 12 BELTS IN EIGHT DIFFERENT WEIGHT CLASSES. BECAUSE THE LEGITIMACY OF SOME OF THOSE BELTS REMAINS IN QUESTION, HOWEVER, THOSE TOTALS DON'T TELL THE WHOLE STORY, SAYS TIM STARKS, BOXING JOURNALIST & AUTHOR OF THE BLOG QUEENSBERRY~RULES.COM.

For the first part of the 20th century, there was only one sanctioning body, the National Boxing Association (later called the World Boxing Association), and it had only eight weight classes, says Robert Rodriguez, an assistant professor of political science at Texas A & M, Commerce, and author of the book *The Regulation of Boxing*. Starting in the 1960s and continuing until today, the regulatory bodies expanded to the point where boxers can hold at least four belts in each class, and those regulatory agencies have split the weight classes from eight to 17.

"It used to be a really big deal. Until the late 1980s, the most titles anyone had won were three," Rodriguez tells *Life's Little Mysteries*. "But it's gotten so confusing; you practically need an encyclopedia to keep track of all these belts. It's pretty ridiculous and pathetic."

A number of fighters, such as Henry Armstrong and Roberto Duran, had won three championship belts before the 1980s. Then, in 1987, Thomas "the Motor City Cobra" Hearns became the first person to win a fourth belt. A year later, he won his fifth. After that, champions just kept on piling up more and more belts.

Most of the boxers who have won multiple titles have done so in the weight classes at or below middleweight. The lower weights have smaller differences between classes, making it easier to move from one to another.

Such was the case with Manny Pacquiao, who began his career as a 112-pound flyweight and who won the 150-pound super welterweight championship against Antonio Margarito in 2010, becoming the first boxer in history to have won belts in eight different weight classes.

"Belts don't make a man," Starks said. "But in Pacquiao's case, they most certainly are a compelling part of his legacy."

by Stuart Fox

Which NFL Records Can Never Be Broken?

In professional sports, records are made to be broken.

There are, however, a few marks considered so untouchable they appear unbreakable. Wilt Chamberlain's 100-point game is an NBA record that has stood for 48 years, and the closest anyone has come to matching it was Kobe Bryant, with 81 points in a 2006 game. Baseball player Cy Young's 511 pitching victories is an even greater statistical anomaly. Considering the nature of modern-day baseball, it is virtually inconceivable that any MLB pitcher will ever come close to this mark.

Unlikely though it may be, it remains possible that those records could fall. Tony Dorsett's 99-yard touchdown run, however, is another matter.

On Monday, Jan. 3, 1983, the Dallas Cowboys great and later pro football Hall of Famer Tony Dorsett ran his way into the NFL record books for all time with the longest run from scrimmage in league history.

Dorsett's 99-yard record run can never be broken. This is because NFL rules call for the game to be played on a field 100 yards long. The yardage begins with the one-yard line, not the zero. Therefore, the longest run possible in the NFL is 99 yards in length.

THE 99-YARD RECORD RUN JAN. 3, 1983, BY DALLAS COWBOYS GREAT TONY DORSETT CAN NEVER BE BROKEN. THIS IS BECAUSE NFL RULES CALL FOR THE GAME TO BE PLAYED ON A FIELD 100 YARDS LONG. THE YARDAGE BEGINS WITH THE ONE-YARD LINE, NOT THE ZERO. THEREFORE, THE LONGEST RUN POSSIBLE IN THE NFL IS 99 YARDS IN LENGTH.

The closest that anyone could come to breaking the record would be to tie Dorsett and share the mark with him. Unless the league changes one of the fundamental parts of the game—the 100-yard field—Tony Dorsett's name will always be found in the pro football record book.

It's important to note the difference between Dorsett's record for the longest run from scrimmage and the longest play, period. The NFL's longest play was a 109-yard missed field goal return by Antonio Cromartie in 2007. That length was possible because when a play includes a kickoff, punt, interception or fumble return, officials measuring the length of the play take into account how far back a player is in the end zone (which is 10 yards long), according to league rules.

That rule does not apply for offensive plays started from scrimmage, such as running or passing plays, so records for those plays will always remain at 99 yards.

In NFL history, 99-yard passing plays are more common than 99-yard running plays. There have been 11 passing plays of that length, the most recent in 2008. But Dorsett's mark remains the only run to go that long, making it a singularly unique achievement.

In the book *Run It! And Let's Get the Hell Out of Here! The 100 Greatest Plays in Pro Football History*, Dorsett describes his famous gallop.

"I just saw a lot of green," Dorsett says. "When I came to the sideline, [Cowboys player personnel director] Gil Brandt said, 'I think that was an NFL record.'"

What's even more impressive about the run is that Dorsett saw all that open space despite the fact his team was missing one player on the field. The Cowboys fullback had mistakenly stayed on the sideline, so Dallas only had 10 men on the field for the historic play. Turns out, it didn't matter.

Dorsett's one regret from that night? "I should've kept the ball."

by Michael Avila

What's the Longest Winning Streak in Any Sport?

ustained excellence in sports is the enduring mark of a champion, which is why winning streaks are so fascinating for fans.

The longest winning streak in an individual sport belongs to Pakistani squash legend Jahangir Khan. A six-time world champion, Khan was dominant in the 1980s—he won 555 consecutive matches from 1981 to 1986.

But when the length of a winning streak is measured in years, instead of in individual contests, two other legendary athletes have an argument for the longest winning streak. Edwin Moses dominated the 400-meter hurdles in track and field for nearly a decade, winning 122 straight races from 1977 to 1987. Moses won the Olympic gold medal in the 400 in 1984 (the U.S. boycotted the 1980 Moscow Olympics) and broke his own world record four times along the way.

Boxer Julio-Cesar Chavez was the victor in 87 consecutive fights between 1981 and 1993, the longest unbeaten streak—13 years—in boxing history.

In professional team sports, the longest winning streak belongs to the NBA's Los Angeles Lakers. The legendary 1971-1972 squad, featuring Hall of Famers Jerry West, Gail Goodrich and Wilt Chamberlain, won 33 straight games, en route to the league title.

The NFL's longest win streak belongs to the New England Patriots, who won 21 games in a row over the 2003 and 2004 seasons.

The Chicago Cubs may be known as baseball's lovable losers for their 102-year World Series drought, but the team also owns the sport's longest winning streak. The Cubbies won 21 straight games in 1935.

It should be noted that the then-New York Giants won 26 games in a row in 1916. Technically, the team had a tie game in the middle of the streak, which interrupted the winning streak. However, Major League Baseball doesn't include ties in its official record, and therefore recognizes the Giants' streak as the longest.

Perhaps the most impressive winning streaks in team sports belong to college programs.

The UCLA men's basketball team, under the legendary coach John Wooden, won 88 consecutive games from 1971 to 1974.

Right behind them is University of Connecticut's women's basketball team, which is currently on a 78-game win streak that just netted the squad their second consecutive NCAA championship.

The Oklahoma Sooners football team under coach Bud Wilkinson won 47 consecutive games from 1953 to 1957.

THE LONGEST WINNING STREAK IN AN INDIVIDUAL SPORT BELONGS TO PAKISTANI SQUASH LEGEND JAHANGIR KHAN. A SIX-TIME WORLD CHAMPION, KHAN WAS DOMINANT IN THE 1980s. HE WON 555 CONSECUTIVE MATCHES FROM 1981 TO 1986.

All of those streaks pale in comparison to the level of excellence reached by the De La Salle high school football team. The California private Catholic school chalked up 151 victories in a row from 1992 to 2003—the team was undefeated for 11 years.

It's not out of the question to suggest that De La Salle's winning streak may never be challenged in team sports, at any level of competition.

by Michael Avila

What's the Most Dangerous Move in Karate?

he 2010 remake of *The Karate Kid* focuses on kung fu, which, like the karate from the original, consists primarily of kicks and punches. But in actual fighting, kicks and punches rank very low on the damage scale, with chokeholds and elbows proving the most dangerous.

The rear neck choke, more widely known as the sleeper hold, poses the greatest risk, says Vitor Ribeiro, a three-time Brazilian jujitsu world champion and instructor at Modern Martial Arts in New York City.

Karate and kung fu, which consist primarily of kicks and punches, do not use this choke hold, but it is found in jujitsu, judo and other grappling-focused disciplines.

In this move, the attacker positions himself behind the victim, wraps his arm around the opponent's neck and cuts oxygen off to the victim's brain. This renders the victim unconscious at first, and can cause death if the choke continues.

> IN JUJITSU'S REAR NECK CHOKE, THE ATTACKER POSITIONS HIMSELF BEHIND THE VICTIM, WRAPS HIS ARM AROUND THE OPPONENT'S NECK AND CUTS OXYGEN OFF TO THE VICTIM'S BRAIN. THIS MOVE RENDERS THE VICTIM UNCONSCIOUS AT FIRST, AND IT CAN CAUSE DEATH IF THE CHOKE CONTINUES.

"Sometimes you can take someone down with a punch or kick, but then the person can get up and come at you again. Someone with one arm can still fight," Ribeiro tells *Life's Little Mysteries*. "When you choke someone and put them to sleep, sometimes they don't get up."

Because of the extreme effectiveness of the rear neck choke, many martial arts have developed countermeasures specifically designed to defeat the move. However, making sure that one's back never faces the opponent is the most effective measure to prevent the maneuver from being performed on you.

In karate, the most dangerous move is simply an elbow to the face. Elbows are harder than fists, and an attack with an elbow is more likely to make contact than a knee or kick attack.

Whereas a punch can lead to a broken fist, an elbow will simply make a solid impact, Ribeiro says.

by Stuart Fox

When Was the First Fantasy Football League Organized?

he Fantasy Sports Trade Association estimates that nearly 18 million people played fantasy football in 2009. The rise in popularity goes hand-in-hand with the continuing national obsession with professional football.

Baseball may be the national pastime, but the NFL is America's most popular sport, according to a Gallup poll, and according to the all-important barometer of television ratings. Fantasy football in recent years has similarly overtaken fantasy baseball as the most popular fantasy game in the United States. But most of today's casual fantasy participants probably don't realize that fantasy football origins date back nearly 50 years.

THE FIRST FANTASY FOOTBALL LEAGUE WAS ORGANIZED IN 1962 IN MANHATTAN, WHEN THREE MEN FROM OAKLAND WERE IN TOWN FOR THE GAMES OF UPSTART NFL COMPETITOR THE AMERICAN FOOTBALL LEAGUE, ACCORDING TO THE NFL.

The first fantasy football league was organized in 1962 in Manhattan, when three men from Oakland were in town for the games of upstart NFL competitor the American Football League, according to the NFL. Bill Winkenbach, a limited partner in the Oakland Raiders, Scotty Stirling, an Oakland Tribune sportswriter, and Bill Tunnell, who worked in public relations for the Raiders, devised the game in a room at what is now the Milfred Plaza Hotel in New York City during the Raiders' annual visit to play East Coast teams. In a 2004 article in the *San Francisco Chronicle*, Stirling credits Winkenbach with coming up with the idea.

Winkenbach also came up with the league's name. The "Greater Oakland Pigskin Prognosticators League" (GOPPL) was not only the first official fantasy football league, but it was also the first to have a little fun with the league name, something that's now become part of the fun for fantasy nuts everywhere.

Once the men returned to Oakland, *Tribune* sports editor George Ross was brought in to help fine-tune their new game. The rules for the first year of the GOPPL were remarkably similar to the current fantasy game. You drafted players who had the highest propensity for scoring touchdowns and gaining yards, same as you do today. The big difference between then and now was the available research.

In 1962, there was no Internet to instantly crunch wide receiver statistics, very few printed football magazines to pore over except for the old Street & Smith preseason guides, and ESPN didn't exist.

The first player ever drafted in the history of fantasy football? That would be future Hall of Famer (and then Oakland Raider quarterback) George Blanda.

The founding fathers of fantasy football never made a dime off their groundbreaking creation. Even more surprising is the fact that, while the game has exploded in popularity in the past decade, Ross and Stirling, the two surviving charter members of the original league, haven't played fantasy football in more than a quarter century. Winkenbach died in 1993, and reportedly played the game until close to the end of his life.

The guys who touched off a phenomenon never saw it coming. They thought all they did was devise a fun, in-season diversion.

"I had no idea it would explode into the kind of mania that exists today," Stirling told the *Fantasy Football Index* in 1994.

Millions of number-crunching football fans in man-caves and offices everywhere owe those trailblazing guys in the Greater Oakland Pigskin Prognosticators League a great debt for making their fall Sundays more competitive, and more fun.

by Michael Fox

Why Is the Length of the Indy 500 Set at 500 Miles?

he length of the iconic Indy 500 auto race was not chosen arbitrarily, but instead rather meticulously.

In 1911, the year of the debut race, the owners of the Indianapolis Motor Speedway—the track that hosts the Indy 500—decided that a seven-hour event would appeal to race fans. That length of time would allow them to arrive at the track in mid-morning and return home by evening. With top speeds of cars at that time ranging between 75 mph (121 kph) and 90 mph (145 kph), the owners set the distance at 500 miles (805 km), or 200 laps around the 2.5-mile (4.0-km) oval raceway.

THE WINNING DRIVER OF THE FIRST INDY-500 RACE, RAY HARROUN, CLOCKED IN AT SIX HOURS, 42 MINUTES AND EIGHT SECONDS. IN 2009, HELIO CASTRONEVES WON THE RACE IN LESS THAN HALF THAT TIME HE FINISHED IN THREE HOURS, 19 MINUTES AND 34 SECONDS.

The winning driver of the first Indy-500 race, Ray Harroun, clocked in at six hours,

---

The following are some quick facts about the Indy 500:

- At 253 acres (102 hectares), the Speedway oval is large enough to encircle Churchill Downs, Yankee Stadium, the Rose Bowl, the Roman Colosseum or Vatican City.

- There is a three-way tie for having the most wins, A.J. Foyt, Al Unser and Rick Mears each have four.

- The closet race happened in 1992. Al Unser Jr. beat Scott Goodyear by just 0.043 seconds.

- Al Unser also has the longest gap between victories, with 17 years separating his 1970 and 1987 wins. When he won in 1987, Unser became the oldest Indy 500 winner in history. Unser was 47 and 360 days old when he won.

(Source: Indianapolis Motor Speedway)

---

42 minutes and eight seconds. In 2009, Helio Castroneves won the race in less than half that time—he finished in three hours, 19 minutes and 34 seconds.

by Michelle Bryner

Which City Has Hosted the Super Bowl the Most Times?

 he 2014 Super Bowl was awarded to the joint bid submitted by the New York Giants and New York Jets, a significant milestone for America's unofficial national holiday, Super Bowl Sunday.

For the first time, the Super Bowl was set to be played in the largest metropolitan area in the country, which also happens to be the No. 1 media market in the United States. The event is expected to provide a $550 million boost to the local economy, says New York Jets Chairman and CEO Woody Johnson.

While the Big Apple is a Super Bowl rookie, for a few other cities, hosting a Super Bowl is practically routine.

Miami has played host to the Super Bowl more times than any other city. Ten Super Bowls have taken place there, the first five at the legendary Orange Bowl stadium (in 1968, 1969, 1971, 1976, and 1979), and the last five at Joe Robbie Stadium (in 1989, 1995, 1999, 2007, and 2010).

Miami is also the only city to host the contest in two consecutive years—it hosted Super Bowls II and III.

> MIAMI HAS PLAYED HOST TO THE SUPER BOWL MORE TIMES THAN ANY OTHER CITY. TEN SUPER BOWLS HAVE TAKEN PLACE THERE, THE FIRST FIVE AT THE LEGENDARY ORANGE BOWL STADIUM (IN 1968, 1969, 1971, 1976 AND 1979), AND THE LAST FIVE AT JOE ROBBIE STADIUM (IN 1989, 1995, 1999, 2007, AND 2010).

Coming in a close second is New Orleans, which has hosted nine Super Bowls (most recently, in 2002). The Louisiana Superdome in that city also holds the distinction of being the single stadium with the most Super Bowls under its belt, with six. (Tulane Stadium hosted New Orleans' first three Super Bowls.) Super Bowl XLVII in 2013 is set to be played at the Superdome, which means New Orleans will then tie Miami as the most prolific Super Bowl host.

Los Angeles has hosted seven Super Bowls, but hasn't done so since 1993. That's because the NFL enacted a rule to only award Super Bowls to cities with a team, and L.A. has been without one since both the Rams and Raiders left town in 1995.

The 2014 game also marks the first time the Super Bowl will be played outdoors in a cold-weather city. Since the first NFL-AFL World Championship Game (the game wasn't called the Super Bowl until Super Bowl III) was played in Los Angeles in 1967, professional football's biggest battle has primarily been waged in warm-weather cities. The few times the Super Bowl has ventured into more frigid territory, such as Detroit and Minneapolis, where the game was played inside the cozy confines of a climate-controlled dome.

The possibility of a snowstorm during the league's marquee event worried some owners, but the NFL built its legacy with classic cold-weather games like the 1967 "Ice Bowl" between the Green Bay Packers and the Dallas Cowboys.

by Michael Avila

Does a Horse's Post Position Affect Its Chances of Winning the Kentucky Derby?

nown as the "fastest two minutes in sports," the Kentucky Derby is the king of all horse races. Up to 20 of the country's fastest 3-year-old thoroughbreds sprint around the mile-and-a-quarter track at Churchill Downs in Louisville, Ky., in hopes of picking up the first jewel in racing's Triple Crown series.

The "Run for the Roses" attracts over $80 million in wagers, and theories of how to pick a winner abound. Of all the variables that could affect the outcome, one of the favorites is the order in which the horses line up at the opening gate, otherwise known as the post position.

STARTING IN 2010, THE SELECTION PROCESS RETURNED TO THE TRADITIONAL BLIND DRAW USED PRIOR TO 1998. IN THIS SYSTEM, THE NUMBER DRAWN WILL BE THE HORSE'S ACTUAL STARTING GATE. SO, THE OWNER WHO DRAWS THE NUMBER 3 GETS GATE 3. THIS PROCESS TAKES AWAY SOME OF THE STRATEGY OF BEING ABLE TO CHOOSE FROM THE AVAILABLE GATES.

Post positions are numbered from one to 20, with No. 1 being on the track's inside rail and No. 20 being the farthest outside. Let's look at how these positions are determined, and which one has historically been the most successful.

From 1998 to 2009, the Derby used a two-tiered drawing system to determine starting positions. In the first drawing, owners drew a number from one to 20, and this number would determine the order in which they could choose their starting position. So, if an owner drew number 3, then he would have third pick as to which starting gate he wanted for his horse. Horses differ in their running styles. Some prefer to be closer to the inside rail while others prefer to be on the outside, where there is more space.

Starting in 2010, the selection process returned to the traditional blind draw used prior to 1998. In this system, the number drawn will be the horse's actual starting gate. So, the owner who draws the number 3 gets Gate 3. This process took away some of the strategy of being able to choose from the available gates. Derby officials cite the declining television coverage of the draw, along with requests from owners and trainers, as reasons for the switch.

Once the post positions are determined and you know where your favorite 3-year-old will be, you may wonder what the odds are of winning from that gate.

Historically, the best position has been the No. 2 post. Out of the 135 previous Derby runs, the horse in this position has won 29 times. Unlike auto racing where the No. 1 position is coveted, horse owners and jockeys usually prefer gates in the No. 2 to No. 10 positions. In these spots, there is less chance of getting pinned along the rail than there is for the No. 1 position, yet they still put the horse close enough to the rail to be inside many other horses at the first turn. An amazing 96 winners have come from the No. 2 to No.10 posts.

In the last 52 years, only two horses have won after starting from outside the No. 16 post. But don't start slamming mint juleps just yet if your horse ends up in the No. 20 post. In 2008, Big Brown, the pre-race favorite, won from that spot after his owners chose that position for him.

by Dan Peterson

How Do You Shoot a Perfect Free Throw?

The free throw is basketball's tool of justice. When one player bumps or knocks another, officials reward the victim with what seems like a chance to score easy points. The clock stops, the other players get out of the way, and the shooter stands centered, just 15 feet from the basket, to calmly put the ball through the net.

It should be a cinch, right? But the best players in men's college basketball only hit about 69 percent of free throws. Even NBA players, the best in the world, only make about 75 percent of them. And these averages have not improved in decades.

Leave it to two mechanical and aerospace engineers to find the best technique for the perfect free throw. Chau Tran and Larry Silverberg, professors at North Carolina State University, studied hundreds of thousands of three-dimensional computer simulations of free-throw trajectories to find the best combination of ball aim, rotation and shooting angle. Here's their formula for sailing a shot through the 18-inch rim.

> AIM FOR THE BACK OF THE RIM. INTERESTINGLY, CHOOSING WHAT SEEMS LIKE A MORE LOGICAL TARGET THE CENTER OF THE BASKET REDUCES ACCURACY BY ALMOST THREE PERCENT. TRY TO LEAVE 2 INCHES BETWEEN THE BACK OF THE RIM AND THE BALL.

First, aim for back of the rim. Interestingly, choosing what seems like a more logical target—the center of the basket—reduces accuracy by almost three percent. Try to leave 2 inches between the back of the rim and the ball.

Next, put about three hertz of backspin on the ball. For those without an engineering degree, this means the ball should spin three full rotations on its way from your hand to the basket. This rate of spin will deaden the ball if it hits the rim, helping it to fall through the hoop.

Finally, release the ball at an angle of 52 degrees to horizontal. The rule of thumb is that, at its highest point, the ball should be less than two inches from the height of the top of the backboard. Coming down at this angle gives the ball the best chance of going through the hoop, even it touches the sides of the rim.

If players get the aim, spin, and angle right, we might finally see the free throw live up to its name.

by Dan Peterson

Why Are Marathons 26.2 Miles Long?

o, you want to have a really long race that eventually will attract the best runners from around the world. Unlike other races with boring names like the "mile" and the "400-meter," with their well-defined distances, your race commemorates an ancient Greek town with an unusual route totaling somewhere around 24 to 26 miles.

Well, if you're Pierre de Coubertin, founder of the International Olympic Committee and the Modern Olympics, that was exactly the plan for the marathon at the 1896 Olympics in Athens.

In a nod to Greek history, the first marathon commemorated the run of the soldier Pheidippides from a battlefield near the town of Marathon, Greece, to Athens in 490 BC. According to legend, Pheidippides ran the approximately 25 miles to announce the defeat of the Persians to some anxious Athenians. Not quite in mid-season shape, he delivered the message "Niki!" (Victory!) then keeled over and died.

So, de Coubertin organized the first official race from the Marathon Bridge to Olympic Stadium in Athens, a distance of about 24.85 miles (40,000 m). Spiridon Louis, a Greek postal worker, won that first race in 2 hours, 58 minutes and 50 seconds, finishing seven minutes ahead of the pack. Of the 25 entrants, only 9 runners hit the finish line.

After 1896, the next few Olympic marathons varied in distance with the idea that as long as all runners ran the same course, there was no need to keep the distance exactly the same.

For the 1908 London Olympics, the course was laid out from Windsor Castle to White City stadium, about 26 miles. However, to locate the finish line in front of the royal family's viewing box, an extra 385 yards was added inside the stadium. Hence the marathon tradition of yelling "God save the Queen" in the last mile.

> THE FIRST MARATHON COMMEMORATED THE RUN OF THE SOLDIER PHEIDIPPIDES FROM A BATTLEFIELD NEAR THE TOWN OF MARATHON, GREECE, TO ATHENS IN 490 BC. ACCORDING TO LEGEND, PHEIDIPPIDES RAN THE APPROXIMATELY 25 MILES TO ANNOUNCE THE DEFEAT OF THE PERSIANS TO SOME ANXIOUS ATHENIANS.

Despite the success of that first race, it took 13 more years of arguing before the International Amateur Athletic Federation (IAAF) adopted the 1908 distance as the official marathon. In fact, of the first seven modern Olympics, there were six different distances.

Today, there are more than 500 organized marathons in 64 countries around the world each year, with more than 425,000 marathon finishers in the United States alone. As many of these veterans will tell you, the first 26 miles are easy—it's that last quarter mile that will kill you.

by Dan Peterson

What's the Story Behind Golf's Green Jacket?

Some golf tournaments give trophies, some give cars. But only one gives its winner a green sports jacket—the Masters.

In an annual tradition that dates back more than 60 years, the previous year's champion helps the new winner put on the fairway-green coat with the logo emblem of the host, Augusta National Golf Club, on the left side. However, like most things at the Masters and Augusta, there are rules for the green jacket.

Augusta National co-founder Clifford Roberts gave every club member a green jacket as the standard dress code at club functions. The official reason was to distinguishmembers from non-members during public tournaments and events. However, unofficial Augusta historians have said the real reason was Roberts was tired of members trying to out-dress each other with fancy jackets. Hence, the great green equalizers to keep egos in check.

In 1949, after winning his first of three Masters championships, Sam Snead was awarded the first green jacket as an honorary member. Since then, the reigning champion is allowed to take his green jacket home with him, but then must return with it the following year to help the new champion slip into his

AUGUSTA NATIONAL CO-FOUNDER CLIFFORD ROBERTS GAVE EVERY CLUB MEMBER A GREEN JACKET AS THE STANDARD DRESS CODE AT CLUB FUNCTIONS TO DISTINGUISH MEMBERS FROM NON-MEMBERS DURING PUBLIC TOURNAMENTS AND EVENTS. IN 1949, AFTER WINNING HIS FIRST OF THREE MASTERS CHAMPIONSHIPS, SAM SNEAD WAS AWARDED THE FIRST GREEN JACKET AS AN HONORARY CLUB MEMBER.

own jacket. In the case of a repeat champion, (there have only been three, Jack Nicklaus, Nick Faldo and Tiger Woods), the current Augusta chairman does the honors.

The previous year's champ also has to leave his jacket behind at Augusta. All of the coats are kept there and may be worn by past winners whenever they visit, as they often do, since they are given a lifetime invitation to play in the tournament.

On the Tuesday evening of each Masters week, there is a room full of green coats at Augusta when a dinner for all past champions is held. Started by Ben Hogan in 1952, only past winners, with a few club VIPs, are invited with the reigning champion getting to pick the menu.

In addition to the stylish clothing, tournament champs also receive a gold medallion (more than 13" in diameter!), a replica trophy like the full-size one kept at Augusta and a sizable check of $1.35 million.

by Dan Peterson

Chapter 9
Tech

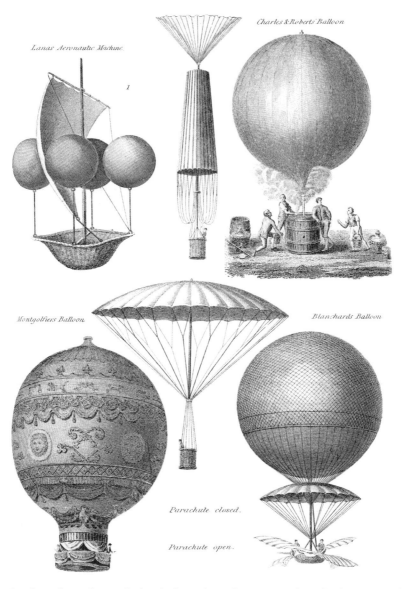

Lanas Aeronautic Machine.

Charles & Roberts Balloon

Montgolfiers Balloon

Blanchards Balloon

Parachute closed.

Parachute open.

Technology has changed the look and performance of such things as the vehicles we drive and the way we conduct business. And we are just scratching the surface of the potential that computers, the internet and smartphones can play in our lives. In this chapter, we talk about some of what makes up the technology we enjoy today.

What Everyday Things Around Us Are Radioactive?

he average American is exposed to about 620 millirem (mrem) of radiation each year, according to the U.S. Nuclear Regulatory Commission (USNRC). This radiation comes from both natural and man-made sources.

Half of our yearly dose comes from natural "background radiation" present in the environment. Most of this comes from radon (an odorless, colorless, gas naturally occurring in the air), and smaller amounts come from cosmic rays and the Earth itself.

The other half of a person's radiation dose each year comes from man-made sources, which can be medical, commercial or industrial, but medical procedures typically account for 96 percent of a person's man-made radiation exposure.

"In general, a yearly dose of 620 millirem from all radiation sources has not been shown to cause humans any harm," according to the USNRC.

So just what around us is contributing to our yearly radiation dose?

Food. All plants and animals contain trace amounts of radioactive potassium-40 and radium-226. In fact, all water contains dissolved radioactive uranium and thorium, according to the USNRC.

However, these amounts are very small. The radiation in all the food and drink a person ingests over a year adds up to about 30 mrem.

The Sun. While Earth's atmosphere does a good job of protecting us from the continuous stream of cosmic radiation striking the planet from the sun and stars, some radiation gets through.

Where a person lives determines the amount of cosmic radiation they are exposed to, as differences in elevation, atmospheric conditions and Earth's magnetic field can alter radiation dosage.

For example, a person living in mile-high Denver gets more than 50 mrem every year, compared with the 26 mrem that a resident of sea-level Key West, Fla., gets, according to the Centers for Disease Control and Prevention. Denver's higher altitude means thinner air, which makes it easier for the sun's UV rays to get through.

> HALF OF A PERSON'S RADIATION EXPOSURE EACH YEAR COMES FROM MAN-MADE SOURCES, WHICH CAN BE MEDICAL, COMMERCIAL OR INDUSTRIAL. MEDICAL PROCEDURES TYPICALLY ACCOUNT FOR 96 PERCENT OF A PERSON'S MAN-MADE RADIATION EXPOSURE, ACCORDING TO THE U.S. NUCLEAR REGULATORY COMMISSION.

Air Travel. High altitudes are also to blame for exposure to cosmic radiation during flights. How much radiation absorbed during a flight depends on the plane's altitude and latitude, and on solar activity.

For a typical cross-country flight in a commercial airplane, a person receives 2 to 5 mrem, less than half the dose received during a chest X-ray (10 mrem), according to the U.S Environmental Protection Agency (EPA).

In addition, a person receives about 0.002 mrem from airport security scans each way, according to the EPA.

Cell Phones. Threats to health from cell phone radiation have been a persistent, though scientifically uncertain, concern for years now. In June, San Francisco voted to become the first U.S. city in which retailers must display the radiation levels emitted by cell phones.

"We are not suggesting people abandon cell phones—we certainly wouldn't—but we suggest that people use cell phones differently by using headsets and that they buy low-radiation cell phones," Olga Naidenko, a senior scientist at the Environmental Working Group, tells *TechNewsDaily*, a sister online magazine to *Life's Little Mysteries*.

Cell phones, as well as radio towers and Wi-Fi networks, emit radio frequency waves, which are absorbed by human tissue and measured using the Specific Absorption Rates (SARs) scale.

Medical X-rays. Because medical procedures make up 96 percent of the average person's exposure to man-made radiation, people should limit the number and types of X-rays they receive. X-ray, mammography and CT (Computerized Axial Tomography or CAT scan) machines all increase a person's dose.

A chest X-ray typically delivers a dose of about 10 mrem, while a full-body CT scan packs a 1,000-mrem punch. A CT scan of the chest delivers 700 mrem, while a scan of the head gives 200 mrem. A dental X-ray gives 1.5 mrem, and an X-ray of a hand or foot delivers 0.5 mrem, according to the USNRC.

by Remy Melina

How Do Fireworks Get Their Colors?

ehind the scenes of the dazzling light shows that spectators "ooh and ahh" at on the Fourth of July are carefully crafted fireworks. Whether red, white and blue fountains or purple sparklers, each firework is packed with just the right mix of chemicals to create these colorful lights.

Inside each handmade firework are small packets filled with metal salts and metal oxides that react to produce an array of colors. When heated, the atoms of each element in the mix absorb energy, causing its electrons to rearrange from their lowest energy state to a higher "excited" state. As the electrons plummet back down to their lower energy state, the excess energy gets emitted as light.

Each element releases a different amount of energy, and this energy is what determines the color or wavelength of the light that is emitted.

THE RECIPE THAT CREATES BLUE INCLUDES VARYING AMOUNTS OF COPPER CHLORIDE COMPOUNDS, WHILE RED COMES FROM STRONTIUM AND LITHIUM SALTS.

For instance, when sodium nitrate is heated, electrons in the sodium atoms absorb the energy and get excited. As the electrons come down from the high, they release their energy, about 200 kilojoules per molecule, or the energy of yellow light, says Chemistry Professor Bassam Z. Shakhashiri at the University of Wisconsin-Madison.

The recipe that creates blue includes varying amounts of copper chloride compounds, while red comes from strontium and lithium salts.

Just like paints, secondary colors are made by mixing the ingredients of their primary-color relatives. A mixture of copper (blue) and strontium (red) makes purple.

by Michelle Bryner

How Does an Atomic Clock Work?

 imekeeping can be as simple as counting "one Mississippi, two Mississippi …" prior to blitzing in backyard football, or tracking the back-and-forth swings of a pendulum in a grandfather clock.

In both cases, the trick is counting the intervals of something that occurs repeatedly with as little variation as possible. A pendulum swing, say, or a "Mississippi" just about equates to a second, the unit of timekeeping that, as we know, comprises minutes and hours.

But even the best mechanical pendulums and quartz crystal-based clocks develop discrepancies. Far better for timekeeping is the natural and exact "vibration" in an energized atom.

When exposed to certain frequencies of radiation such as radio waves, subatomic particles called electrons that orbit an atom's nucleus will "jump" back and forth between energy states. Clocks based on this jumping within atoms can therefore provide an extremely precise way to count seconds.

It is no surprise then that the international standard for the length of one second is based on atoms. Since 1967, the official definition of a second is 9,192,631,770 cycles of the radiation that gets an atom of the element cesium to vibrate between two energy states.

Inside a cesium atomic clock, atoms are funneled down a tube where they pass through radio waves. If this frequency is just right—9,192,631,770 cycles per second—then the cesium atoms "resonate" and change their energy state.

A detector at the end of the tube keeps track of the number of cesium atoms reaching it that have changed their energy states. The more finely tuned the radio wave frequency is to 9,192,631,770 cycles per second, the more cesium atoms that reach the detector.

WHEN EXPOSED TO CERTAIN FREQUENCIES OF RADIATION SUCH AS RADIO WAVES, SUBATOMIC PARTICLES CALLED ELECTRONS THAT ORBIT AN ATOM'S NUCLEUS WILL "JUMP" BACK AND FORTH BETWEEN ENERGY STATES. CLOCKS BASED ON THIS JUMPING WITHIN ATOMS CAN THEREFORE PROVIDE AN EXTREMELY PRECISE WAY TO COUNT SECONDS.

The detector feeds information back into the radio wave generator. It synchronizes the frequency of the radio waves with the peak number of cesium atoms striking it. Other electronics in the atomic clock count this frequency. As with a single swing of the pendulum, a second is ticked off when the frequency count is met.

The first quality atomic clocks made in the 1950s were based on cesium, and such clocks—honed to greater precisions over the decades—remain the basis used to keep official time throughout the world.

In the United States, the top clocks are maintained by the National Institutes of Standards and Technology (NIST) in Boulder, Colo., and the United States Naval Observatory (USNO) in Washington, D.C.

The NIST-F1 cesium atomic clock can produce a frequency so precise that its time error per day is about 0.03 nanoseconds, which means that the clock would lose one second in 100 million years.

Super-accurate timekeeping is integral to many elements of modern life, such as high-speed electronic communications, electrical grids and the Global Positioning System (GPS)—and of course knowing when your favorite television show comes on.

by Adam Hadhazy

What's Genetic Engineering?

Genetic engineering is the process of using technology to change the genetic makeup of an organism—be it an animal, plant or a bacterium.

This can be achieved by using recombinant DNA (rDNA), or DNA that has been isolated from two or more different organisms and then incorporated into a single molecule, according to the National Human Genome Research Institute (NHGRI).

Recombinant DNA technology was first developed in the early 1970s, and the first genetic engineering company, Genentech, was founded in 1976. The company isolated the genes for human insulin into *E. coli* bacteria, which allowed the bacteria to produce human insulin.

After approval by the U.S. Food and Drug Administration (FDA), Genentech produced the first recombinant DNA drug, human insulin, in 1982. The first genetically engineered vaccine for humans was approved for the treatment of hepatitis B by the FDA in 1987.

Since the 1980s, genetic engineering has been used to produce everything from a more environmentally friendly lithium-ion battery to infection-resistant crops such as the HoneySweet Plum. These organisms made by genetic engineering, called genetically modified organisms (GMOs), can be bred to be less susceptible to diseases or to withstand specific environmental conditions.

But critics say that genetic engineering is dangerous. In 1997, a photo of a mouse with what looked like a human ear growing out of its back sparked a backlash against using genetic engineering. But the mouse was not the result of genetic engineering, and the ear did not contain any human cells. It was created by implanting a mold made of biodegradable mesh in the shape of a 3-year-old's ear under the mouse's skin in order to demonstrate one way to produce cartilage tissue in a lab, according to the National Science Foundation.

While genetic engineering involves the direct manipulation of one or more genes, DNA can also be controlled through selective breeding. Precision breeding, for example, is an organic farming technique that includes monitoring the reproduction of species members so that the resulting offspring have desirable traits.

AFTER APPROVAL BY THE U.S. FOOD AND DRUG ADMINISTRATION (FDA), GENENTECH PRODUCED THE FIRST RECOMBINANT DNA DRUG, HUMAN INSULIN, IN 1982. THE FIRST GENETICALLY ENGINEERED VACCINE FOR HUMANS WAS APPROVED FOR THE TREATMENT OF HEPATITIS B BY THE FDA IN 1987.

A recent example of the use of precision breeding is the creation of a new type of rice. To address the issue of flooding that was wiping out rice crops in China, Pamela Ronald, a professor of plant pathology at the University of California-Davis, developed a more flood-tolerant strain of rice seed.

Using a wild species of rice that is native to Mali, Ronald identified a gene, called Sub1, and introduced it into normal rice varieties using precision breeding to create a hardier rice strain which can withstand being submerged in water for 17 days, rather than the usual three.

Researchers hope the Xa21, as the new rice strain is called, will join the ranks of other GMOs currently being commercially grown worldwide, including herbicide-tolerant or insect-resistant soy, cotton and corn, Ronald says.

For farmers in China, the world's top producer and consumer of rice, being able to harvest enough of the crop to support their families is literally a matter of life and death. Because Ronald used precision breeding rather than genetic engineering, she hopes the rice will be accepted by genetic engineering critics.

"The farmers experienced three- to five-fold increases in yield due to flood tolerance," Ronald says. "This rice demonstrates how genetics can be used to improve the lives of impoverished people."

by Remy Melina

How Does a Virus Infect Your Computer?

hough they're not a living thing like you and me, computers can get "sick" from viruses, too.

A computer virus is a software program designed to replicate itself and spread to other machines. In most cases, the program is "malicious," meaning its purpose is to cause the computer to malfunction in some way.

In general usage, the term "computer virus" includes all forms of "malware," or malicious software.

Instead of sniffles and a fever, some common symptoms of a computer viral infection are slow performance, data loss and system crashes, all of which can make people using the machine feel ill, as well.

VIRUSES CAN ENTER YOUR COMPUTER ANY NUMBER OF WAYS, SUCH AS VIA AN EMAIL ATTACHMENT, DURING FILE DOWNLOADS FROM THE INTERNET OR EVEN UPON A VISIT TO A CONTAMINATED WEBSITE.

Yet many technological diseases were designed to remain hidden on a computer and not alert their users, so malware-infected machines may spread silently.

Since Elk Cloner, the first computer virus, left its lab in 1981, millions more have been created by human programmers who get a kick out of sabotaging others' computers.

"There is always something new," says Peter Szor, an independent researcher and former engineer at Symantec Corporation, a maker of antivirus software and author of *The Art of Computer Virus Research and Defense*. Symantec and other virus labs often see more than 30,000 unique malware programs on a single day.

The sinister programs often work by associating themselves with a legitimate program that, when activated, also "execute," or run, the virus' code.

Viruses can enter your computer any number of ways, such as via an email attachment, during file downloads from the Internet or even upon a visit to a contaminated website.

Digital Germs. Just as bacteria and fungi cause illnesses in people, computers can get diseases from other infectious agents besides viruses, including computer worms, Trojan horses and spyware.

Unlike viruses, worms do not have to attach themselves to a program in your computer and may not damage files on an infected computer. Instead, worms often slow down computer networks by eating up bandwidth, or your computer's ability to process data, as the malware replicates and spreads.

Trojan horses, on the other hand, do not self-replicate. Instead, these programs act as the sneaky means for a hacker to gain access to someone's computer to send out spam emails or steal passwords.

Spyware programs monitor a computer user's activity, such as websites they visit, without the user knowing it. They may cause unsolicited advertisements to pop up, or they may steal sensitive information such as credit card numbers.

A whole range of antivirus software is available to prevent and eradicate these malware infections.

"Antivirus programs are evolving to keep up with new threats," Szor says. "My recommendation to users today is to buy the most recent version of the products."

by Adam Hadhazy

How Do Solar Sails Work?

While rocket fuel has provided the energy for most space travel so far, solar energy may provide the boost for spaceships in the future. Just like cloth sails harness the wind, giant reflective sheets called solar sails can harness the sun's energy. These sheets could save fuel and provide maneuverability, but they cannot function deep in space.

Solar sails work by capturing the energy from light particles as they bounce off a reflective surface, according to the U.S. Department of Energy. Each light particle has momentum, and when it strikes a reflective surface, it imparts that momentum to the reflective sheet, just like a collision of two billiard balls.

As billions of light particles hit the sheet, they push the sail strongly enough to move a spacecraft. Over time, the solar particles could keep pushing a spaceship faster and faster, allowing it to attain very high speeds, according to scientists at Argonne National Laboratory.

> UNLIKE ROCKET PROPULSION, WHICH RELIES ON A FINITE QUANTITY OF FUEL, SOLAR SAILS HARNESS THE VIRTUALLY INFINITE PROPULSIVE POWER OF THE SUN'S LIGHT, ACCORDING TO NASA. THIS LIMITLESS ENERGY SOURCE COULD ALLOW SPACESHIPS EQUIPPED WITH SOLAR SAILS TO HOVER AND MANEUVER IN FASHIONS TOO COSTLY FOR SHIPS RELIANT ON FUEL-BASED PROPULSION SYSTEMS.

The sails can be as large as football fields, but are 40 to 100 times thinner than a sheet of paper, according to NASA. Inflatable booms provide the sheets with rigidity and tether the solar sail to a spacecraft.

Unlike rocket propulsion, which relies on a finite quantity of fuel, solar sails harness the virtually infinite propulsive power of the sun's light. This limitless energy source could allow spaceships equipped with solar sails to hover and maneuver in fashions too costly for ships reliant on fuel-based propulsion systems.

However, solar sails do have their limitations. At distances beyond the orbit of Mars in our solar system, the sun becomes too faint to push a solar sail, a phenomenon that limits the use of solar sails in deep space.

The solar panels on some satellites have been used as rudimentary solar sails, but no country had launched a spacecraft that relies primarily on solar sails for propulsion until 2010, when both the Japanese Aerospace Exploration Agency (JAXA) and the American Planetary Society were scheduled to launch solar sail probes.

The Japanese probe, called IKAROS, was designed to travel to Venus with scientific equipment. The U.S. LightSail-I was designed to circle the Earth to test solar sail technology.

The concept of a solar sail dates back almost 400 years. Johannes Kepler, the astronomer best known for calculating the elliptical orbits of the planets, observed solar radiation that creates a comet's tail. Even then, he realized that a sail could harvest that force just as terrestrial sails trap wind power to propel ships.

by Stuart Fox

How Does a Microwave Oven Work?

ercy Spenser was conducting radar experiments during World War II when he leaned up against a microwave-emitting tube and accidentally melted the candy bar in his pocket. Eureka. His dry cleaners were furious, but Spenser quickly understood the sweeter implications of the event, and he went on to patent the first microwave heating device.

The secret to his sticky mess? Let's zap some lunch and find out.

The frozen burrito in your microwave oven sits in an electromagnetic field, bombarded on all sides by high-frequency microwaves. Free water molecules (along with some fats and sugars) absorb the microwaves, and the resulting vibrations cause friction between molecules (i.e. heat). Because not all the water in your burrito has frozen (due to the presence of other chemicals, like salt), heat is generated in those pockets of free molecules sooner than in frozen areas. That's why your burrito sometimes comes out unevenly heated.

> WHY CAN'T YOU WRAP YOUR MICROWAVABLE MEAL IN ALUMINUM FOIL? METAL BLOCKS THE HIGH-ENERGY PARTICLES OF THE ELECTROMAGNETIC FIELD, MAKING FOR MORE TROUBLE THAN A MELTED CANDY BAR.

Why can't you wrap your microwavable meal in aluminum foil? Metal blocks the high-energy particles of the electromagnetic field, making for more trouble than a melted candy bar.

by Ben Mauk

How Do They Build Underwater Tunnels?

 unnels tend to get short shrift when we mete out marvels of engineering. Those that dare to dunk beneath waterways are particularly impressive feats of construction.

Modern underwater tunneling begins by constructing an immersed tube within a pre-dug trench on the river or sea floor. To do this, prefabricated sections of steel tube are floated into position and are strategically sunk into the trench. This technique was first used in 1903 for construction beneath the Detroit River. America also claims the longest tunnel of any kind. The New York City West Delaware water-supply tunnel runs 105 miles (169 km).

MODERN UNDERWATER TUNNELING BEGINS BY CONSTRUCTING AN IMMERSED TUBE WITHIN A PRE-DUG TRENCH ON THE RIVER OR SEA FLOOR. TO DO THIS, PREFABRICATED SECTIONS OF STEEL TUBE ARE FLOATED INTO POSITION AND ARE STRATEGICALLY SUNK INTO THE TRENCH.

But if you want to drive your car under some serious seabed, go abroad. The Seikan Tunnel, which connects Japan's main island of Honshu with the northern Hokkaido, measures 33.4 miles (53.8 km), of which 23.3 miles (14.3 km) lie underwater.

by Ben Mauk

How Do Post Office Machines Read Handwritten Addresses?

either snow nor rain nor scribbled zip code stays these couriers and their computer counterparts from the swift completion of their appointed rounds.

The United States Postal Service (USPS) began researching remote computer readers (RCRs) for handwritten addresses in 1983. At the time, the technology required to scan and understand human scrawl simply did not exist.

Not until Christmas of 1997 did the USPS and the University of Buffalo's Center for Excellence in Document Analysis and Recognition (CEDAR) deploy its first handwritten address-reading prototype, which rejected 85 percent of envelopes and correctly identified the address in only 10 percent of those it read with a 2 percent error rate.

> THE UNITED STATES POSTAL SERVICE BEGAN RESEARCHING REMOTE COMPUTER READERS FOR HANDWRITTEN ADDRESSES IN 1983. AT THE TIME, THE TECHNOLOGY REQUIRED TO SCAN AND UNDERSTAND HUMAN SCRAWL SIMPLY DID NOT EXIST.

Humans read and comprehend with an ease that belies the immense difficulty of computer pattern recognition. The challenge is one of the central problems in artificial intelligence, so even the prototype's 2 percent reading rate was viewed as a great success.

"That Christmas alone we saved several thousand dollars for the Post Office," Sargur Srihari tells *LiveScience*, a sister online magazine to *Life's Little Mysteries*. Srihari founded CEDAR and led the early research on large-scale RCRs.

Today, a large majority of letters sent through the post office are read and sorted entirely by computer. Current reading success rates are above 90 percent.

The process begins when a single envelope is scanned into a digital image. Initial algorithms locate the destination address on the envelope (as opposed to the return address), then parse this address block into discrete lines, and those lines into words. Finally, the software is left with the street number, street name, city, state and zip code.

Actual recognition begins with the zip code and street number. "Numbers are easiest to read," Srihari says, "because they are usually well-formed compared to letters, and there's only 10 numerals."

The program takes these number-values and searches through a database of about 120 million U.S. addresses, emerging with a short list of possible candidates. Then, the computer compares the individual letter features of the handwritten street name to the candidates. "It's a tricky business," Srihari says, "but you can usually recognize a few key features [of the address words]."

"Each word gets a confidence rating. We go through all possible street names, and find the highest confidence value."

The letter is then shipped, first to the correct city, then to the nearest post office. There, the letter is scanned by computer and filed into the appropriate position in a carrier's stack, so that the first human eyes to examine the envelope are those of the postal carrier approaching your mailbox.

by Ben Mauk

How Does Cloning Work?

loning may invoke an image of an army of identical cows or sheep churned out factory-style, but in actuality, the process is much more laborious.

The term "cloning" generally applies to a process more technically known as somatic cell nuclear transfer. DNA from the cell of an adult animal (take cows, for example), called the "donor," is extracted from the cell (usually a skin cell taken in a biopsy) and inserted into an egg cell from another cow. The egg cell has had its nucleus removed so that it will read and duplicate the DNA of the donor cell.

The newly created embryo is then zapped with electricity so that it starts multiplying until it becomes a blastocyst (a small clump of cells that forms after an egg is fertilized), which is then implanted into a surrogate mother. The resulting newborn will be an identical genetic replica to the donor cow.

Cows have been cloned more than other animals because obtaining eggs from the cow is slightly easier than for swine, says geneticist Bill Muir of Purdue University, an author of a 2002 National Academy of Sciences report on the scientific concerns of animal biotechnology.

> IN CLONING, DNA FROM THE CELL OF AN ADULT ANIMAL (TAKE COWS, FOR EXAMPLE), CALLED THE "DONOR," IS EXTRACTED FROM THE CELL (USUALLY A SKIN CELL TAKEN IN A BIOPSY) AND INSERTED INTO AN EGG CELL FROM ANOTHER COW. THE RESULTING NEWBORN WILL BE AN IDENTICAL GENETIC REPLICA TO THE DONOR COW.

Cloning differs from other methods of artificial breeding, such as in vitro fertilization because it uses adult cells instead of embryos.

by Andrea Thompson

Why Do Batteries Go Bad?

 here's a reason behind that expiration date on a fresh package of batteries. Because batteries generate energy using a chemical reaction contained inside the battery cell, they use up energy, even if they haven't yet been snapped inside a remote control or toy.

Most batteries have a long shelf life that varies depending on their type and size, but they weaken over time due to the way they're constructed. Each battery contains electrodes, which are strips of metal tape coated with an oxide (a combination of oxygen and another chemical element) and rolled up like a jelly roll. Certain parts of batteries corrode over time, leaving them less effective or completely unusable.

> MOST BATTERIES HAVE A LONG SHELF LIFE THAT VARIES DEPENDING ON THEIR TYPE AND SIZE, BUT THEY WEAKEN OVER TIME DUE TO THE WAY THEY'RE CONSTRUCTED. EACH BATTERY CONTAINS ELECTRODES, WHICH ARE STRIPS OF METAL TAPE COATED WITH AN OXIDE (A COMBINATION OF OXYGEN AND ANOTHER CHEMICAL ELEMENT) AND ROLLED UP LIKE A JELLY ROLL.

In a recent study, scientists at Ohio State University (OSU) took apart spent batteries and used infrared thermal imaging technology to determine weaknesses in each electrode. They inspected problem spots using scanning microscopes, and found the finely-structured microscopic materials on the electrodes, which allow batteries to rapidly charge and discharge, had become corroded.

They also found that the breakdown of lithium in a battery hinders the transfer of an electric charge between electrodes.

"We can clearly see that an aged sample versus an unaged sample has much lower lithium concentration in the cathode," says study researcher Giorgio Rizzoni. "It has essentially combined with anode material in an irreversible way."

During testing, Rizzoni and other researchers charged and discharged commercially-available batteries thousands of times over months of testing, in a variety of conditions designed to mimic how batteries are used by hybrid and all-electric vehicles. Some were tested in hot temperatures like those in Arizona, while others were tested in colder conditions that mimicked Alaskan weather.

Judging from the test results, the researchers theorize, but cannot yet prove, that the coarsening of the cathode (the "positive" end) may be behind the loss of lithium. Proving their theory correct would be a step towards manufacturers making batteries more durable with longer lifetimes.

by Life's Little Mysteries *Staff*

Chapter 10
Weird

In our final chapter, we provide explanations for everyday phenomena such as how popcorn pops and how scent travels. This chapter also includes the unexplained and the just plain spooky.

Can Bad Memories Be Erased?

any people think a memory is like a video, as if it were a perfect record of events to be replayed over and over again in the mind. But scientists have learned how very unlike a video our memories are. Because memories are subject to suggestion and change over time, they are also finding ways that we might be able to edit certain types of memory, the way we do a home movie.

Specifically, they are studying how to edit memories of fear. In 2000, researchers at New York University discovered they could erase a fear-filled memory in rats by shocking them and then reminding them of the fearful shock while treating them with a chemical that inhibits the creation of proteins in the brain.

The theory behind this and other experiments on animals is that a memory requires the creation of proteins when it first forms in the brain (a process called consolidation), and it creates those proteins again every time it's recalled (reconsolidation).

The NYU researchers guessed that the very act of remembering destabilizes a memory, causing it to be changed or muted. And the results of their experiments and others support this hypothesis.

From Rats to Humans. Treating humans with most of the methods used on rats isn't safe, but researchers from NYU have recently reported being able to create a similar effect in humans by using a non-invasive technique called extinction training.

In a 2009 NYU experiment, human subjects were given an electric shock while viewing an image to give them a fear memory associated with the image. A day later, they were shown the image again, which should have spurred the memory to become unfixed in the brain and susceptible to erasure.

During this "reconsolidation" window, subjects were repeatedly shown the same image but without any shocks. According to the researchers, this extinction treatment was able to banish the fearful memory, even when tested a year later.

Play, Pause and Delete. So far, only these fear-specific memories have been shown to be affected by such editing. Fear memories and other highly emotional recollections involve a different part of the brain—the amygdala—than more run-of-the-mill memories like your grocery list or the birthdays of your family members, according to the NYU research.

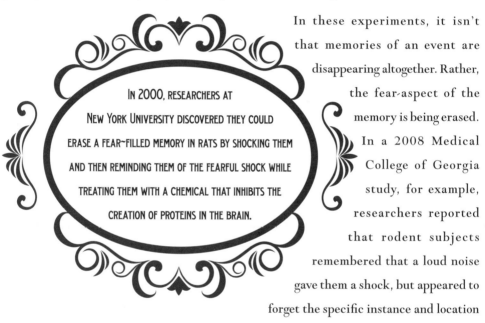

IN 2000, RESEARCHERS AT NEW YORK UNIVERSITY DISCOVERED THEY COULD ERASE A FEAR-FILLED MEMORY IN RATS BY SHOCKING THEM AND THEN REMINDING THEM OF THE FEARFUL SHOCK WHILE TREATING THEM WITH A CHEMICAL THAT INHIBITS THE CREATION OF PROTEINS IN THE BRAIN.

In these experiments, it isn't that memories of an event are disappearing altogether. Rather, the fear-aspect of the memory is being erased. In a 2008 Medical College of Georgia study, for example, researchers reported that rodent subjects remembered that a loud noise gave them a shock, but appeared to forget the specific instance and location of the shock when treated with a chemical that inhibited their brains.

In the recent NYU test on humans, the memory of seeing the image remained, but the fear associated with it was changed or deleted.

by Molika Ashford

Why Do Couples
Start to Look Like Each Other?

hile you may be familiar with the old saying, "opposites attract," in reality, what the heart wants is someone who resembles its owner—and that resemblance increases the longer two lovebirds stay together.

University of Michigan psychologist Robert Zajonc conducted an experiment to test this phenomenon. He analyzed photographs of couples taken when they were newlyweds and photographs of the same couples taken 25 years later.

The results show that the couples had grown to look more like each other over time. And, the happier the couple said they were, the more likely they were to have increased in their physical similarity.

Zajonc suggests that older couples looked more alike because people in close contact mimic each other's facial expressions. In other words, if your partner has a good sense of humor and laughs a lot, he or she will probably develop laugh lines around the mouth—and so will you.

> COUPLES GROW TO LOOK MORE LIKE EACH OTHER OVER TIME. AND, THE HAPPIER THE COUPLE SAY THEY ARE, THE MORE LIKELY THEY ARE TO INCREASE IN THEIR PHYSICAL SIMILARITY.

Evidence has also shown that men and women may be initially attracted to partners with similar personalities. In 2006, scientists at the University of Liverpool asked participants in a study to view individual photos of men and women to judge their personalities. The participants did not know who in the photos was married to whom, but the couples that had been together the longest were judged to have more similar personalities. "Possessing personality traits that are attractive may be causal in making a face attractive," the researchers concluded.

It turns out that we may be hard-wired to fall in love with people sporting DNA that is similar to our own in some ways. In a study of twins, University of Western Ontario scientists found that not only did the study participants tend to pick partners with similar genes; the spouses of the identical twins were also more alike than the spouses of non-identical twins.

Couples look more like each other over time because in some ways they already are like each other.

by Amber Angelle

How Do Magnets Work?

 hysicists have both a large-scale and a small-scale understanding of how magnets function. However, some phenomena that underlie magnetism continue to elude scientific explanation.

The large-scale magnetism, like the kind observable in bar magnets, results from magnetic fields that naturally radiate from the electrically charged particles that make up atoms, says Jearl Walker, a physics professor at Cleveland State University and coauthor of the widely used textbook *Fundamentals of Physics*. The most common magnetic fields come from negatively charged particles called electrons.

Normally, in any sample of matter, the magnetic fields of electrons point in different directions, canceling each other out. But when the fields all align in the same direction, like in magnetic metals, an object generates a net magnetic field.

"Every electron generates a magnetic field, but they only generate a net magnetic field when they all line up. Otherwise, the electrons in the human body would cause everyone to stick to the refrigerator whenever they walked by," Walker says.

Currently, physics has two explanations for why magnetic fields align in the same direction: a large-scale theory called "classical physics," and a small-scale theory called "quantum mechanics."

According to the classical theory, magnetic fields are clouds of energy around magnetic particles that pull in or push away other magnetic objects. But in the quantum mechanics view, electrons emit undetectable, virtual particles that tell other objects to move away or come closer.

Although these two theories help scientists understand how magnets behave in almost every circumstance, two important aspects of magnetism remain unexplained: why magnets always have a north and south pole, and why particles emit magnetic fields in the first place.

> Normally in any sample of matter, the magnetic fields of electrons point in different directions, canceling each other out. But when the fields all align in the same direction, like in magnetic metals, an object generates a net magnetic field, says Jearl Walker, coauthor of the textbook, Fundamentals of Physics.

"We just observe that when you make a charged particle move, it creates a magnetic field and two poles. We don't really know why. It's just a feature of the universe, and the mathematical explanations are just attempts of getting through the 'homework assignment' of nature and getting the answers," Walker says.

by Stuart Fox

Is the Amityville Horror House Really Haunted?

 he home at 112 Ocean Ave., in Amityville, N.Y., is perhaps the most famous haunted house in the world, known to countless horror fans as the setting for *The Amityville Horror*. It's also currently for sale for $1.15 million.

But don't go looking for it—the current owners don't want you to find it. Previous owners, none of whom said they experienced anything spooky or supernatural, have remodeled it so that the signature quarter-moon windows are no longer there. They also changed the house numbers to thwart annoying curiosity seekers; infamous address no longer exists.

The ghost story began in 1974, when six members of a family were killed in that house by their youngest son, Butch DeFeo. The house was sold the following year to George and Kathy Lutz, who moved in with their three children.

Soon after, the Lutzes said they encountered terrifying supernatural forces. A ghost ripped doors from hinges and slammed cabinets closed, noxious slime oozed from the ceilings, and demonic faces and swarms of insects threatened the family.

THE GHOST STORY BEGAN IN 1974, WHEN SIX MEMBERS OF A FAMILY WERE KILLED IN THAT HOUSE BY THEIR YOUNGEST SON, BUTCH DEFEO. THE HOUSE WAS SOLD THE FOLLOWING YEAR TO GEORGE AND KATHY LUTZ, WHO MOVED IN WITH THEIR THREE CHILDREN.

The Lutzes told their story to a writer named Jay Anson, who published *The Amityville Horror: A True Story*. It quickly became a best-seller, and a hit horror film with the same name spawned nearly a half-dozen sequels. It's a scary story that has spooked millions of people. But is it true?

Researchers who double-checked claims made by the Lutzes and Anson found numerous holes in the Amityville story. Researcher Rick Moran, for example, compiled a list of more than 100 factual errors and discrepancies between their story and the truth. Over and over, both big claims and small details were refuted by eyewitnesses, investigations and forensic evidence. Still, the Lutzes stuck to their story and reaped tens of thousands of dollars from the book and the film rights.

Eventually Butch DeFeo's lawyer admitted that he, along with the Lutzes, "created this horror story over many bottles of wine." The house was never really haunted; the terrifying experiences that the Lutzes described that were later embellished by Anson and other writers were simply made up.

The Amityville Horror Hoax House may cost $1.15 million on the market today, but ghosts and demons aren't included.

by Benjamin Radford

Can You Really Die in Your Nightmares?

es Craven's horror movie *A Nightmare on Elm Street* (1984) remains one of the most popular horror movies of all time. But for all its outlandish content, a real disease called sudden unexpected nocturnal death syndrome (SUNDS) inspired the movie, Craven says. SUNDS strikes otherwise healthy young people dead in their sleep, not unlike a certain claw-handed villain in the Elm Street movies.

In SUNDS, which is genetic disease, the body fails to properly coordinate the electrical signals that cause the heart to beat, says Matteo Vatta, an assistant professor of cardiology at the Baylor College of Medicine in Houston. The disease primarily strikes young adult men, especially those of Southeast Asian descent.

"The heart can be normal for quite some time, and then it may stop unexpectedly," Vatta tells *Life's Little Mysteries*. "Usually, the heart stops at night, and in Southeast Asia [the condition] once caused more deaths amongst young males than car accidents."

> In SUNDS, which is genetic disease, the body fails to properly coordinate the electrical signals that cause the heart to beat, says Matteo Vatta, an assistant professor of cardiology at the Baylor College of Medicine in Houston. The disease primarily strikes young adult men, especially those of Southeast Asian descent.

The deaths occur at night because the heart beats more weakly when people sleep. When the heart slows down for sleep, the electrical problems that cause SUNDS become more pronounced, overtake the body's ability to regulate its own heart beat and send the heart into a deadly spasm.

There have been some theories that link the onset of SUNDS to the stress caused by nightmares, but no scientific studies have shown a correlation between SUNDS deaths and the content of dreams.

Currently, there is no effective treatment for SUNDS and no clear reason why it tends to affect Southeast Asians more frequently than other groups. And the syndrome is very difficult to detect, even with a dedicated electrocardiograph reading.

Doctors in the United States and Europe first recognized the disease among refugees who were fleeing the Vietnam War, according to a Center for Disease Control and Prevention report. As those refugees began settling in the United States in the late 1970s and early 1980s, mysterious stories of apparently healthy Southeast Asian men dying in their sleep, and others who refused to sleep from fear of SUNDS, began appearing in newspapers across the country. And a cinematic dream was born.

by Stuart Fox

Why Does Popcorn Pop?

 ithin minutes, a teardrop-shaped kernel no larger than a pea can magically mushroom into a fluffy treat that's at least 35 times its original volume.

The tasty secret: water.

Each popcorn kernel contains a hard outer shell and a starchy inside surrounding a dab of water. When the kernels are heated to about 450°F, the pocket of water turns into steam and expands within the tough casing. Like blowing up a balloon, as more and more steam forms, the pressure against the outer shell increases. When the shell can no longer contain the building pressure, it finally gives way with the classic pop. The kernel turns inside-out, revealing the softened starch that makes up the white spongy part of your favorite movie snack.

by Michelle Bryner

What Is Ball Lightning?

itnesses describe ball lightning as fist-size floating spheres of fire that spin, hover mid-air and sometimes explode. But despite accounts stretching back hundreds of years, scientists still aren't sure what causes this spooky phenomenon—or even if it truly exists.

One of the earliest documented reports of ball lightning came from the events of a stormy Sunday in 1638. A parish church in Devonshire, England, went up in flames and some of the people inside were killed.

Since then, there have been thousands of reported sightings of ball lightning. These mysterious orbs have been seen floating around outdoors, in buildings and even on ships and airplanes. Contemporary accounts tend to be less dramatic than the parish church tale: In general, the worst damage is some singed clothing or furniture.

> ONE OF THE EARLIEST DOCUMENTED REPORTS OF BALL LIGHTNING CAME FROM THE EVENTS OF A STORMY SUNDAY IN 1638. A PARISH CHURCH IN DEVONSHIRE, ENGLAND, WENT UP IN FLAMES AND SOME OF THE PEOPLE INSIDE WERE KILLED.

Perhaps the strongest evidence for ball lightning's existence is that scientists may have recreated it—or something very much like it—in a lab.

In a study published in the journal *Physical Review Letters*, researchers at the Federal University of Pernambuco in Brazil reported using electricity to vaporize tiny wafers of silicon. The result was blue- or orange-white spheres the size of ping-pong balls that hovered around for as long as eight seconds.

The result gave credence to the theory that ball lightning is the result of a lightning strike on silica-rich soil. The vaporized silica, the theory goes, condenses into nanoparticles and is bound together by electrical charges. It glows hot because of a chemical reaction between the silicon and oxygen in the air.

But this theory doesn't explain all reported ball lightning sightings, such as those on airplanes. Other researchers have floated theories for ball lightning ranging from miniature black holes left over from the Big Bang to visual hallucinations caused by epileptic seizures, but the silica theory remains the only lab-tested hypothesis. Out in the real world, these rings of fire remain a mystery best suited for dark and stormy nights.

by Stephanie Pappas

Is the Bermuda Triangle Really Dangerous?

It's been called the Devil's Triangle, Limbo of the Lost and the Twilight Zone, but it is most famously known as the Bermuda Triangle.

The semi-triangular area surrounded by Bermuda, Puerto Rico, and the tip of Florida is known for its voracious appetite for planes and boats. The legend began at 2:10 p.m. Dec. 5, 1945, when, reportedly, experienced aviators lifted off on a routine training mission, in supposedly crystal-clear weather. Upon becoming disoriented, the pilots of Flight 19 radioed for help and then disappeared.

Bizarre explanations for this and other vanishing acts include: aliens hiding under the sea, a portal leading to another dimension, and ship-size methane gas bubbles.

There is a logical answer to the disappearances, however. The Triangle is heavily traveled and proportionally sees no more frequent accidents than other areas. The region is vulnerable to unpredictable storms. And, according to the Navy, the Gulf Stream there "is extremely swift and turbulent and can quickly erase any evidence of a disaster." Finally, the sea in that area is up to 30,000 feet deep.

As for Flight 19, the pilots were actually trainees, and the weather was far from crystal clear that day.

> THE LEGEND BEGAN AT 2:10 P.M. DEC. 5, 1945, WHEN, REPORTEDLY, EXPERIENCED AVIATORS LIFTED OFF ON A ROUTINE TRAINING MISSION, IN SUPPOSEDLY CRYSTAL-CLEAR WEATHER. UPON BECOMING DISORIENTED, THE PILOTS OF FLIGHT 19 RADIOED FOR HELP AND THEN DISAPPEARED.

by Michelle Bryner

Do Hair and Nails Keep Growing After Death?

As creepy as a "yes" would be, the answer is maybe an even creepier "no."

After death, the human body dehydrates, causing the skin to shrink back to expose the part of the nails and hair that was under the skin, causing them to simply appear to grow.

by Life's Little Mysteries *Staff*

Why Do Some Clovers Have Four Leaves?

he leaves of clover plants are said to hold the luck o' the Irish when they sport four leaves. This myth likely arose because four-leaf clovers are rare finds—the result of an equally rare genetic mutation in the clover plant.

There are about 300 species in the clover genus Trifolium, or trefoil, so named because the plants usually have three leaves, or technically, leaflets. The ones you typically find in North America are white clovers (*Trifolium repens*).

Typically all clover plants feature leaves that have three leaflets on them—legend has it that St. Patrick used this so-called shamrock as a symbol of the Holy Trinity. But occasionally the genetics of the clover result in the rare four-leaflet variety, and sometimes even higher-numbered leaves.

ACCORDING TO THE *GUINNESS BOOK OF WORLD RECORDS*, THE MOST LEAVES EVER FOUND ON A CLOVER ARE 18. THIS MANY-LEAFED SPECIMEN WAS FOUND BY SHIGEO OBARA OF JAPAN ON MAY 25, 2002.

"The 4-leaf (technically, 4-leaflet) and higher-leaflet variants are caused by rare genetic mutations," biologist Kenneth Olsen of Washington University in St. Louis tells *Life's Little Mysteries*.

According to the *Guinness Book of World Records*, the most leaves ever found on a clover are 18. This many-leafed specimen was found by Shigeo Obara of Japan on May 25, 2002.

by Andrea Thompson

Can You See a Sonic Boom?

The breaking of the sound barrier is not just an audible phenomenon. In fact, Mach I can be beautiful.

The visual counterpart to a sonic boom, which sometimes but not always accompanies the breaking of the sound barrier, has also been seen with nuclear blasts and just after space shuttle launches, too. A vapor cone was photographed as the Apollo I I moon-landing mission rocketed skyward in 1969.

The phenomenon is not well studied. Scientists refer to it as a vapor cone, shock collar, or shock egg, and it's thought to be created by what's called a Prandtl–Glauert singularity.

Here's what scientists think happens:

At sea-level pressure in 59°F (or 15°C) air, sound travels 760 mph (1,223 kph). When moving at subsonic speeds (greater than Mach I), an aircraft's pressure disturbances (sound waves) are generally distributed in all directions. Sounds are waves of disturbance in the atmosphere, so their velocities depend on air temperature and pressure. Upon breaking the sound barrier, the pressure field of the aircraft extends from the rear of the plane in a Mach cone—a shock wave that builds and causes a sonic boom. That much is well understood.

> THE VISUAL COUNTERPART TO A SONIC BOOM, WHICH SOMETIMES BUT NOT ALWAYS ACCOMPANIES THE BREAKING OF THE SOUND BARRIER, HAS ALSO BEEN SEEN WITH NUCLEAR BLASTS AND JUST AFTER SPACE SHUTTLE LAUNCHES, TOO. A VAPOR CONE WAS PHOTOGRAPHED AS THE APOLLO II MOON~LANDING MISSION ROCKETED SKYWARD IN 1969.

At the same time, a layer of water droplets gets trapped between two high-pressure surfaces of air, scientists say. In humid conditions, condensation can gather in the trough between two crests of the sound waves produced by the jet. This effect does not necessarily coincide with the breaking of the sound barrier, although it can.

For the record, on Oct. 14, 1947, USAF Major Charles "Chuck" Yeager flew into aviation history by piloting a Bell XS-1 research plane to supersonic speeds. These days NASA is flying unmanned aircrafts at close to Mach 10 velocity.

> THE MORE LIKELY SUBSTANCES ARE DISSOLVED IN WATER, THE HEFTIER THEIR ODOR.

The origins of the Mach number stretch back before humans ever took flight, to 1887, when Austrian physicist Ernst Mach established his principles of supersonics. His famous Mach number is the ratio of an object's velocity to the velocity of sound, relative to the local environment.

by Life's Little Mysteries *Staff*

How Does Scent Travel?

To get to your nose, a rosy smell rides the wind. Unfortunately, stinky scents travel the same route.

Substances that easily vaporize release airborne molecules. In contrast, nonvolatile substances such as glass do not give off smelly molecules.

Ever notice that the stench of a garbage pile is stronger on a hot and humid day? The conditions increase molecular volatility.

In addition, the more likely substances are dissolved in water, the heftier their odor.

Wafts of air carry scent-filled molecules to sensory cells in the nose.

The nose is a powerful sensor. A 2007 study published in the journal Psychological Science found that scents so faint people couldn't even smell anything still had an effect on people's emotions. Even at undetectable doses, scents floating in the air can manipulate our reactions.

by Corey Binns

Why Can't We Reach the End of the Rainbow?

You'll never swim out to the horizon, and you'll never reach a rainbow's end. The visibility of both require distance between the object and observer.

Rainbows consist of water droplets being struck by sunlight in a certain way. Round, transparent drops of water refract and internally reflect some sunlight towards the observer. Different wavelengths of light refract (change angles) at different angles, so the white light of the sun is parsed into an orderly band of colors.

A high density of waves emerges traveling in the direction of the least deviation from the entry angle, and it is these waves that create the rainbow.

> As these insubstantial pageants are but light and water, don't go searching for the touchdown spot. The optical phenomenon depends upon you being situated a distance from the droplets with the sun at your back.

As these insubstantial pageants are but light and water, don't go searching for the touchdown spot. The optical phenomenon depends upon you being situated a distance from the droplets—with the sun at your back.

by Ben Mauk